D1170697

Advance Praise for

DELICIOUS DECEMBER

"What a treat! Not only does Peter Rose provide us with an enjoyable history of Santa Claus but also with seasonal recipes of treats to enjoy while reading. Now, when asked about St. Nicholas, Sinter Claes, or Santa Claus I can safely refer people to a reliable source."

— Charles T. Gehring, Director, New Netherland Research Center

"Delicious December is really two great books in one, revealing the little-known Dutch origins of American Christmas traditions, while also bringing into American kitchens dozens of lovely, festive Dutch recipes that few American cooks have ever heard of. Like a wonderful Christmas present, this book gives us historical insights we have long wished for—as well as delicious surprises we did not even know to ask for."

— Stephen Schmidt, food historian and author of
Master Recipes: A New Approach to the Fundamentals of Good Cooking

"Peter Rose knows more about Dutch life and lore than anyone I've ever come across, and she's done it again! This exuberant excursion into the world of Christmas reveals the Dutch roots of many of our holiday traditions and, best of all, provides us heaps of richly tempting recipes to make everyone's favorite season even more memorable."

— Nach Waxman, owner, Kitchen Arts & Letters, Inc.

"A must-read for those interested in the origin of Santa and lovers of feel-good holiday season food."

— Rob de Vos, Consul-General of
the Kingdom of the Netherlands to New York

DELICIOUS DECEMBER

DELICIOUS DECEMBER

How the Dutch Brought Us Santa, Presents, and Treats

A Holiday Cookbook

Peter G. Rose

To my Mother for the past

To Don for the present

To Peter Pamela for the future

Published by
State University of New York Press, Albany

Printed in the United States of America

EXCELSIOR EDITIONS
is an imprint of
State University of New York Press

For information, contact State University of New York Press, Albany, NY
www.sunypress.edu

Production, Laurie Searl
Marketing, Fran Keneston

Library of Congress Cataloging-in-Publication Data

Rose, Peter G.
Delicious December : how the Dutch brought us Santa, presents, and treats : a holiday cookbook / Peter G. Rose.
pages cm. — (Excelsior editions)
Includes index.
ISBN 978-1-4384-4913-5 (hardcover : alk. paper) 1. Christmas cooking. 2. Cooking, Dutch. 3. Dutch Americans—Social life and customs. I. Title.
TX739.2.C45R67 2013
641.5'686—dc23
2013003407

10 9 8 7 6 5 4 3 2 1

Contents

Foreword

I CAN STILL SMELL THE FIREPLACE at my parents' house. The sounds of wood rustling, the fragrance of the hot cocoa my mother made while my sister and I were filled with anticipation of what was to come: the lovely sweet treats and, of course, the presents. We sang our traditional songs knowing *Sinterklaas* would soon arrive and, we hoped, fulfill our dreams.

This tradition might sound all too familiar to an American audience, but this night took place not on December 24, but on December 5, the date the Dutch celebrate *Sinterklaas*, known as Saint Nicholas or later, Santa Claus. The title of the book says it all; the Dutch brought Santa to the United States and the Americans took over numerous Santa Claus traditions from the Dutch celebration of *Sinterklaas.*

Russell Shorto writes in his 2004 international bestseller *The Island at the Center of the World* how the Dutch seasonal routines and rituals tended to prevail and how difficult it must have been for the Swedish, French, and German families who inhabited New Netherland to see the Dutch children receive their treats on the saint's feast day. As the Dutch tradition was adopted and became aligned with Christmas, *Sinterklaas*, Shorto writes: "began his American odyssey."

In the Netherlands, *Sinterklaas* is, after all these years, still the most valued Dutch holiday. It is a tradition, along with many other Dutch customs that took hold in the first settlements of New Netherland that later became part of New York State. To this day, Americans eat cookies after the Dutch *koekjes* instead of the English biscuits, and even the well-known term *Yankees* has a Dutch origin.

Holidays and cultural traditions are only a small part of the rich exchange between the United States and the Netherlands, beginning some 400 years ago, when Henry Hudson discovered this remarkable piece of land.

Peter Rose has been able to capture a part of this long tradition of exchange in her culinary stories and recipes. *Delicious December* focuses on one of the ways the Dutch settlers influenced and enriched the United States. I would like to congratulate her on her book, which combines extensive research on the Dutch tradition in the United States with a unique celebration of the mutual holidays.

ROB DE VOS

Consul-General of the Kingdom of the Netherlands to New York

Acknowledgments

MY SINCERE THANKS TO CONSUL-GENERAL of the Kingdom of the Netherlands to New York, Rob de Vos, for writing the foreword to this book. It is wonderful and heartwarming to have friends you can always count on. Steve Schmidt is such a friend. I thank him most sincerely for not only helping me with some of the recipes, but especially for proofreading the first three chapters. His wise input has made this a better book. My heartfelt thanks also to Dr. Charles T. Gehring, director of the New Netherland Research Center, for all his help over many years.

Debra Thimmesch used her artist's skills in gilding the large Saint Nicholas cookie and did a beautiful (and ever so patient) job as the illustration shows. She helped me as well with figuring out the decoration of the letter cookies. Ron McClary joined me one day and together we deep-fried for hours to make the New Year's specialties. My Catholic friend, Fran Dowling, explained the veneration of saints to me and lent me various books to help me understand the subject.

It has been a pleasure to work again with James Peltz, Laurie Searl, and Fran Keneston of SUNY Press. Their thoughtful and artistic advice has been invaluable.

My nephew Wouter van Vloten helped me immeasurably by finding missing information, interesting and relevant websites, and above all by allowing me to use the image of the Saint Nicholas icon in his collection for this book.

We celebrate Saint Nicholas together every year and always have a wonderful, hilarious time. I want to thank my son-in-law Jason Harris for letting me use one of his funny poems in this book. My deep thanks go also to my beloved daughter Peter Pamela who will continue the tradition. My husband Don not only patiently put up with another year of book writing, but also was an enormous and vital help in recipe testing. As always, Don makes everything possible.

Introduction

IN THE NETHERLANDS, the celebrating begins early in the delicious month of December with *Sinterklaasavond*, the feast of Saint Nicholas and the main gift-giving occasion (rather than Christmas as is the custom in the United States). On December 5, schools, offices, and businesses close early so everyone has a chance to do last-minute gift wrapping or rhyming of poems that accompany the presents. Saint Nicholas actually arrives in Amsterdam two weeks or more prior to the evening's festivities (and his arrival is also a celebration in itself). He needs this time to shop, prepare his horse to ride on the rooftops, and distribute presents to those children and adults "who have been good." The naughty ones will get the *roe*—switches for spanking.

The December 5 celebration begins after dinner, which is generally a hurried, unimportant affair of a sandwich and a cup of soup or leftovers. When everyone is together in one room, the celebration usually starts with the singing of *Sinterklaas liedjes* (Saint Nicholas songs). Then there is banging on the door, and when the door is opened, *pepernoten,* little spice cookies the size of small nuts are suddenly scattered in the hallway. The children will be too busy picking them up to notice the large sack left in front of the door. Everyone exclaims: "*Sinterklaas* was here!" The sack is quickly brought inside, and the evening begins.

Coffee, tea, and hot cocoa are the usual drinks, and Bishop (hot, spiced wine) is served later to the adults, but the most important part of the refreshments are the sweets. There will be little spice cookies and larger ones called *speculaas,* small marzipan "potatoes," chocolate, and coarse fondant. Lots of it.

Why am I so fond of such a simple celebration and have such good memories of it? It is the anticipation and the *gezelligheid,* that elusive Dutch word that means coziness, conviviality, and sociability all in one. I am not the only one; you can ask any Dutch person about their memories of the occasion and they will smile and start to reminisce.

A year or so ago, reminiscing is exactly what six of us Dutch women did when we were together in a New York apartment. Some of us had lived in America thirty or forty years, others only ten years or less. All of us remember our Dutch native language as well as our Dutch customs and celebrations. We agreed that it is difficult to explain *Sinterklaasavond* to Americans, especially since no meal is connected to it. Americans are used to having a Thanksgiving or Christmas feast, and Jewish holidays also are highlighted by a meal. This is why I explain the Dutch festivity as an ongoing "dessert party."

We sat together and talked about all those sweet goodies—the almond paste filled puff pastry; the marzipan in various shapes; and the chocolate, not to mention the spiced honey cakes, some chewy and the others crisp; and for those who really like sweets, creamy fondant made with sugar and heavy cream (see fondant recipe, page 28). We all came from different parts of the Netherlands but had the same memories: how when we were small we were a bit scared of Saint Nicholas, who "always knew if you had been good or bad." One of us said she had even wet her bed the night before the celebration because she was so worried that Saint Nicholas might tell her she had been naughty—or that he might even decide she would have to go home with him in the bag of Black Peter, his helper, as the ultimate punishment.

We remembered that in schools, offices, or in large families, lots were drawn to decide for whom you would buy a present, make a poem, and surprise. (The same thing is done here at Christmas time, commonly known as "a secret Santa.") The surprise, which is pronounced "surpreese," is meant to disguise the present in such a way that the giver remains anonymous (all gifts are from *Sinterklaas*), and it is a real surprise. One person told us how sorry she had been (and still is to this day) for her neighbor. He really wanted a new typewriter (yes, this was in the days of typewriters). His wife had managed to get an empty typewriter box, loaded it down with some heavy stuff to get the right weight, and put a chocolate typewriter inside—with a poem of course. He was so happy, until he opened the box. Most surprises are funny or clever: a very big box for big hoop earrings and a poem that explains how big those earrings really are; or a first-aid kit to hide a tube of hand lotion. All are meant to be silly, innocent little jokes.

As you can see, the presents for the occasion are not big. There is no sign of the abundance that is part of the gift giving in America. Hanny Veenendaal, our hostess that afternoon, still had her diary from 1965 in which she described all the gifts she had received that year: at the top of the list was a necklace, then two drip candles (the type we used to stick in wine bottles), knee socks and long stockings, a box with pennies, a box of cookies, a chocolate letter, a molded honey cake, a molded sugar animal, and a little bear of chocolate. Her list ends with the heartwarming question: "Don't you think that's a lot?"

When I asked my six friends if they still celebrated, I found that my little family and I are the only ones who still celebrate with presents, poems, the traditional sweets, and drinks—and that the others do not celebrate the holiday at all anymore. Ever since our daughter studied abroad and could not come home for December 5, we moved our festivities to Christmas Eve and celebrate Christmas the next day. Therefore, I have also changed the menu: no leftovers, or soup and a sandwich for us. I make a little buffet of *huzarensla,* (see recipe, 81), a salad of potatoes, cooked vegetables as well as diced cucumber and apples, served with dishes of cooked shrimp and deviled eggs. Cold cuts, bread and butter round out the meal, with all the customary sweets waiting for dessert.

Our afternoon of reminiscences ended with a song: "See, yonder comes the steamboat..." a traditional *Sinterklaas* song. Verse after verse we remembered, and then we started singing one song after another. Smiling and in full voice, the six of us sat there

and sang those songs so happily associated with our Dutch youth. I came home with tears in my eyes.

This book is the book I have always wanted to write because writing it gave me a chance to relive my wonderful memories of the festive month of December. In it, I talk about the secular Saint Nicholas celebration and its recipes, and Dutch specialties for Christmas and New Year's. In addition, I have included some recipes from the 1683 edition of *De Verstandige Kok*, which I translated as *The Sensible Cook* (1989). The book shows the varied cuisine of the time period when New Netherland was settled. I also share recipes for savory cookies and party treats as well as more menus and recipe ideas for the parties that might happen between the feast days. This book is divided into two parts: Part I consists of three chapters that discuss the history of Saint Nicholas, how he was brought to America where he became Santa, and what other changes have taken place here as well as in the Netherlands. Part II consists of 111 recipes that are easy to make and easy to love. I wish you a Delicious December!

Replica of seventeenth-century cake board with image of Saint Nicholas

PART I

Saint Nicholas in the New World

Nineteenth-century icon of Saint Nicholas, surrounded by twelve pictures of his life and miracles. He is shown in the center wearing the traditional garments of an Eastern Orthodox Bishop. Christ and Mary are portrayed on either side of his head. The images from left to right: 1. the birth of Saint Nicholas; 2. his baptism; 3. healing a woman's hand while still a youngster; 4. at school; 5. becoming a deacon; 6. being ordained as a bishop; 7. appearing to Emperor Constantine in a dream; 8. visiting three innocents in jail; 9. saving a shipwrecked sailor; 10. delivering a kidnapped boy to his parents; 11. his death and burial; 12. the transfer of his body to Bari in 1087.

The History of Saint Nicholas

THE LEGEND OF SAINT NICHOLAS, who later would become Santa, is like an elaborate piece of embroidery with many intertwined threads, threads that start in the fourth century and wind their way through history to the present day, not only in Asia Minor and Europe, but also in North and South America.

The man who became known as Saint Nicholas is believed to have been born in Patara in present-day Turkey. He became the bishop of nearby Myra, now called Demre, a town near the port of Andriake, on the south coast of Asia Minor between the islands of Rhodes and Cyprus. He is said to have died on December 6 and was declared a saint between 340 and 350. December 6 as "Nicholas Day" is part of the Roman calendar. Saints' days are generally celebrated on the day of their death and rebirth in heaven. In Byzantine icons he is portrayed as a bishop dressed in the vestments of the Eastern Orthodox Church, wearing an omophorion, a band of brocade decorated with crosses worn about the neck and shoulders, symbolizing his spiritual and ecclesiastical authority (see opposite page). In Western portrayals he is clad as a Roman Catholic bishop with a red bishop's garment, miter, and crozier.

Nicholas was the son of well-to-do parents. According to legend, he was pious from a very early age and was attributed with many miracles throughout his life. I must point out though, that Saint Nicholas's first encomium or the description of the life of a saint, was written between 814 and 840, nearly 500 years after his death, which explains the confusion in the details of his life and historians' reluctance to confirm some incidents or even to say with certainty that he was a single individual rather than a composite of several who went by the same name.

By the sixth century, word of his miracles had reached Greece, and in the ensuing centuries spread to Russia, southern Italy and western Europe. Tales of Saint Nicholas saving sailors can be found after the eighth century, and it was sailors who helped spread his fame as Nicholas churches appeared, ringing the seaports of the Mediterranean, Aegean and Adriatic seas.

The practice of substituting Christian saints for pagan gods and Christian festivals for pagan ones was encouraged by early church officials, and continued over time. According to Charles W. Jones in his wonderfully detailed book, *Saint Nicholas of Myra, Bari, and Manhattan: Biography of a Legend,* this eastern saint is assumed to have taken the place of the Greek god Poseidon in the heart of pagans. However, instead of causing shipwrecks as Poseidon was wont to do, he saved sailors from them. Poseidon was also the god of horses and is purported to have ridden the "spume of the cresting wave, as if

Seventeenth-century Dutch painter Cornelis de Vos'
The Charity of Saint Nicholas

it were a horse," Jones writes. Perhaps this is where Saint Nicholas acquired his faithful steed that we see him ride in contemporary Dutch celebrations. Then again, some Dutch historians think the tale of Saint Nicholas and his horse come from Germanic folklore.

The Dutch tradition of Saint Nicholas bestowing gifts anonymously at night appears to hark back to his most famous miracle. It is said that a poor father had no dowries for his three daughters and agonized over the fact that they might end up unmarried, and perhaps, even prostitutes. After hearing the sad tale, Saint Nicholas delivered a bag of gold one night for the oldest daughter and then returned twice more with sacks of gold for the other daughters when they came of age. He is often portrayed with three gold balls, which represent the bags, as an attribute, or a visual way of identifying saints, and we see him pictured in this way in frescoes and sculptures. Seventeenth-century Dutch painter Cornelis de Vos (1584–1651) illustrated the entire miracle tale in *The Charity of Saint Nicholas* (see pages 4-5). He portrays it as if it happened in seventeenth-century Holland. On a dark night, Saint Nicholas is seen dropping a bag of gold through the window while the three young women are busy with their sewing and lace making and the father is reading. It was such a famous miracle that in medieval times it was often performed as a rhymed miracle play. Another famous story, later made into a miracle play, tells how Saint Nicholas saved three boys who had been killed, cut up, and their body parts salted away in a pickle barrel. He restored them to life and punished the evil killer. The boys in a barrel are also frequently seen in portrayals of Saint Nicholas, and even found on a Dutch seventeenth-century carved cake board (see page xiv, 22).

In other stories as well, Saint Nicholas is shown as a gift giver, whether of dowries or of life. I believe it is the purity of the anonymous gift—expecting nothing more in return than knowing one has done a good deed—that sustains his legend. However, there is a pedagogical quality to his giving, and perhaps another reason for his fame. It is illustrated by part of a song Dutch children sing every year. Such songs, which tell the stories of various miracles, date back as far as the eleventh century and were first written in Latin then later in the languages of the countries where Saint Nicholas day celebrations took place. The song's lyrics, in part: *wie zoet is krijgt lekkers, wie stout is de roe,* in English translates into good [children] get sweets, naughty ones get switches for spanking. This sentiment is duplicated in Clement Moore's famous poem *A Visit from Saint Nicholas.* The authorship of that poem is now disputed (see page14).

Through art, song, poetry, and religion, the fame of Saint Nicholas continued to steadily spread. A Saint Nicholas church was founded in Kiev as early as 882. By 988, Christianity became the Russian state religion, and Saint Nicholas was often portrayed in icons of the Eastern Orthodox Church (see page 2).

Around the first millennium, pilgrimages, which would cancel the guilt of sins committed, became very popular. Myra was on the way to the Holy Land, and pilgrims would stop to worship at the tomb of Saint Nicholas. Pilgrims were inveterate collectors of relics, and one such relic might have been vials of the oily liquid that oozed from his tomb and were said to have healing qualities, as both Jones and Seal relate in their books.

On April 11, 1087, Saint Nicholas's remains were taken or you could say stolen from the church in Myra by merchants from Bari. On May 9, 1807 (Translation Day in the

Roman Catholic Church calendar; translation means removal/stealing of bones), he was interred in Bari in the province of Apulia, Italy, where he still can be found in the Basilica Pope Urban II dedicated to him in 1089. Ever since then, May 9 is celebrated in Bari and a vial of the oily liquid is collected from the tomb as a sign of Saint Nicholas's continued protection of the city, as told by Jeremy Seal in *Nicholas: The Epic Journey from Saint to Santa Claus.* Also of note is that the city of Venice disputes that all of Saint Nicholas's bones are in Bari. Venetians claim that during the Crusades, pilgrims to Myra brought some of his remains to Venice, where they are housed in the Saint Nicholas Church on the Lido.

By 1089, Christianity and the legend of Saint Nicholas had spread throughout Europe from Russia, to Italy, France, England, Germany and the Low Countries of present-day Belgium, the Netherlands and Luxemburg. His fame was spread by returning Crusaders as well as troubadours, and he became the main character of medieval miracle plays and the subject of songs/hymns sung in the churches. From his earliest days, Nicholas was more of a secular personality than most other saints. He was never cloistered, and unlike many saints, he was not a martyr. He was seen as a worldly problem solver as in the dowry story, and appeared to have spent his life as a good Christian helping others. He therefore became a folk hero, an all-purpose intercessor, and the patron of a wide variety of professions from button makers, solicitors, sailors, and firemen, to merchants, florists, and tanners. Above all he was the patron saint of children, scholars, and schools. This is probably why he is generally referred to in Dutch as *Sinterklaas,* a more homey, folksy name, and a contraction of the Dutch words *Sint Heer Claes, or* Saint Squire Claes, which is short for Nikolaas, and not the more church-like *Sint Nikolaas.* This is perhaps also why his day was reduced in stature. According to the St. Nicholas Center, a very informative website, "the 1969 Roman Catholic calendar revision did not remove Saint Nicholas," but his feast day on December 6 is "not obligatory under Roman Catholic law."

Luther denounced the mediation of saints as contrary to the teachings of the Bible and taught his followers to pray directly to God. During the Reformation, as iconoclasts smashed paintings, sculptures, and stained glass windows depicting the saints in churches, the celebration of Saint Nicholas moved from the church to the home, where gift giving became central to the festivities. In the Dutch Republic during and after the Eighty Years' War (1568–1648) with Spain, stringent laws and regulations were introduced against saints' feasts and other Roman Catholic commemorations. Historian Simon Schama described them in his book, *The Embarrassment of Riches,* as "acts of petty suppression." Schama told how the city of Delft banned the sale of gingerbread men in 1607 and that the magistrates of Amsterdam prohibited the sale of dolls and molded cookies, while a statute in the city of Arnhem of 1662 forbade children to put their shoe by the chimney and the baking of molded spice cookies. J. J. Schilstra, the foremost Dutch authority on cookie molds, holds how *Sinterklaas* images were carved to look like an ordinary tradesman in disguise. Yet the celebration of Saint Nicholas Day with its treats and gifts for children—*het Kinderfeest* or "Children's Feast"—endured, not only in the Netherlands but, as we will see, in the next chapter in New Netherland as well.

The Feast of Saint Nicholas by Jan Steen

2

The Dutch Bring Saint Nicholas to the New World and He Becomes Santa Claus

SAINT NICHOLAS CAME TO THE NEW WORLD with Christopher Columbus, who gave Saint Nicholas Harbor and Saint Nicholas Mole in Haiti their names. A mole is a massive stone breakwater or pier to enclose a harbor. A slightly later explorer founded Saint Nicholas Ferry in Florida, which we know today as Jacksonville. But the more important story of Saint Nicholas in the New World has to do with the Dutch.

The Netherlands was and still is a seafaring nation and a nation of traders. By the first decade of the seventeenth-century, the Dutch had discovered a southern sea route around Africa to Asia and the Spice Islands and consequently founded the East India Company. They were following in the wake of Portugese navigator Vasco da Gama and subsequent Portugese and Spanish explorers. Because the Dutch were at war with Spain and Portugal, they were looking for safer routes to the Far East. Thus Willem Barent and Henry Hudson were commissioned to find a route to the northeast over Siberia that would avoid contact with Spanish and Portugese maritime activity to the south. Hudson also thought he could find a route to the west, but as we know, he failed though he made it possible for the Dutch to claim the huge watershed called New Netherland, a vast area between New England and Virginia stretching from the Connecticut River to the Delaware Bay and comprising the present-day states of New York, New Jersey, Delaware, parts of Maryland, Pennsylvania, and Connecticut. In 1621, the Dutch government granted the Dutch West India Company a charter with exclusive trading rights in the Western Hemisphere. In 1626, the company purchased the island of Manhattan from the Lenape Indians. The only document of this acquisition is a letter by Pieter Jansen Schaghen dated November 5, 1626. In 2009, as part of the Hudson Quadricentennial Celebration, this letter was displayed at South Street Seaport Museum as "the birth certificate of the City of New York." In 1664 the English took over New Netherland, and with the exception of a brief interlude in 1673–74, when the Dutch took New Netherland back, the area remained in British hands until the American Revolution. Yet, in only seven brief decades, those persistent settlers managed to entrench their culture in this country.

Twelve thousand assorted documents remain from the Dutch period. Since 1974, they have been translated by the New Netherland Project, now the New Netherland Research Center in Albany, New York. The documents are not the only remnants of the Dutch period. Every day we eat dishes that can be traced back to the early Dutch settlers, who brought with them well-established and well-documented food ways. Among the many documents remaining in Dutch archives is a menu of 1631, considered an example of the daily fare of the masses in the Netherlands at the time and the food of our early settlers.

It includes such dishes as wheat bread soup, salted meats, ground beef with currants, fish, cabbage, beans, peas, bread, and cumin cheese. Pancakes and porridges were common dishes as well.

The Dutch brought not only their foodstuffs and methods of preparation, but also their customs and celebrations. As discussed in chapter 1, during and after the Reformation celebrations of saints were strongly discouraged and forbidden by the Dutch Reformed Church as "papist." Yet, the celebration of Saint Nicholas continued, probably in part because he was less of a saint but more of a folk hero. Through the painting on page 8 by Jan Steen and the drawing below by Cornelis Dusart, we can see that the saint's celebration in the 1600s was a gift-giving occasion for children. Children in the Steen painting have put their shoe by the chimney to receive goodies and gifts, a tradition that goes back as far as the 1400s when shoes were put out on December 6 in churches. Wealthy people would drop money in the shoes to be divided among the poor. In the Steen painting, portraying a family together, the little girl has received a John the Baptist doll and a basket with candies and baked goods, more of which we see in the foreground, including a long spiced honey cake. The pedagogical aspect of the event is clearly seen in the fact that the big boy (who apparently had been naughty) received the *roe*, switches

The Saint Nicholas Celebration by Cornelis Dusart

for spanking, in his shoe. Fortunately, there is always Grandma who comes to the rescue with a coin or a present for the boy as she beckons him to look in the cupboard bed in the back. The other children standing by the chimney sing a song to *Sinterklaas* to thank him for all the goodies he brought them. On a table to the right of the Mother figure we see a dish of sweets and fruit, and leaning against it is a *duivekater*, a holiday bread, discussed below.

In the colored drawing by Dusart an extended family is also portrayed. The grandfather sits close to the fire and smokes a pipe—note the filled stocking, which still hangs on the mantle—while the grandmother is still in the cupboard bed, smiling and gesturing at the wonderful treats *Sinterklaas* has brought. The children are clearly overjoyed with their gifts. In this depiction, they have hung their stockings by the chimney instead of placing shoes. The girl to the right near the well-worn broom has on her arm a basket full of baked goods, which includes a long Deventer spiced *koek* cake. She also seems to be holding a doll. The city of Deventer, situated in the northeast Netherlands, has been known for these spice cakes since the Middle Ages, and they are still made there today. The child also proudly holds a *duivekater*, (see recipe, page 28) baked throughout the month of December at least until Epiphany or January 6. It is a rich, buttery, often lemon-flavored bread made from refined white wheat flour, which was far more expensive than the whole-grain flours used in everyday breads at the time. *Duivekaters* were dispensed to the poor by the deacons of the Reformed Church in Brooklyn, so we know they were made in New Netherland as well.

The little boy by the chair in the middle of the drawing holds up a *kolf* stick. *Kolf* was played on land as well as on skates on the ice. It was called *kolven op 't ijs,* a form of ice hockey. It was played in New Netherland as well, both on streets and on the Hudson River in wintertime. Charles Gehring, who translated most of the 12,000 documents remaining from the Dutch period, found an ordinance from the mid-1600s prohibiting *kolf* being played in Beverwijck, now Albany, because of broken windows and injuries to inhabitants. On the chair stands a shallow basket with more treats. It contains apples and pears as well as more *koek* and bread. Various fruits, nuts, and baked goods are associated with the *Sinterklaas* celebration, not only seasonal fruits such as apples and pears, but also oranges from the Mediterranean area. The oranges may be connected to the popularity of Prince William of Orange, as well as his two sons, who fought valiantly in the Eighty-Years War. Or they may have been meant to suggest that the golden balls that are among St. Nicholas's attributes and that inspired the anonymous giving are the essence of the celebration.

In Dusart's drawing, spiced hard gingerbread dotted with whole almonds is leaning against the back of the chair. Recipes for both hard and soft gingerbread (see recipe, page 41) are found in hand-written cookbooks recorded by descendants of the early Dutch settlers and were handed down from generation to generation. All the treats portrayed in the drawing may well have been purchased at the lively Saint Nicholas markets held during the weeks before the big day and where baked goods and toys such as dolls or *kolf* sticks were for sale. Not all of the treats for the occasion are portrayed in Dusart's drawing, however.

Marzipan treats

Also associated with the celebration are *pepernoten*—we know them as pfeffernusse—spiced cookies rolled into small balls or chunks. Also part of the holiday are large spiced cookies made in wooden molds and carved into male or female figures, known as *vrijers* or *vrijsters*. They were so named because Saint Nicholas, in giving dowries to the three maidens, was seen as a *huwelijksmaker* or "wedding maker." Young men and women would present these to each other as signs of affection. Other items not pictured in the drawing include molded sugar animals and marzipan, which are still part of the celebration today. Professor Johanna Maria van Winter, a medievalist and retired professor at the University of Utrecht in The Netherlands explained to me that those items hark back to times before the Reformation when during church-imposed periods of fasting, such as Advent—December 5 falls during Advent—the eating of four-footed animals and their products was forbidden. Marzipan and coarse fondant were colored and shaped to look like sausages or formed in molds to resemble pigs, cows or horses.

The fact that the celebration continued in the New World becomes quite clear when we look at a baker's account, dated March 1676, in the Van Rensselaer Manor Papers held at the New York State Archives, early evidence that the Dutch brought the Saint

Maria van Rensselaer's account with Wouter Albertsz. Van den Uythoff, de backer (the baker), 1676.

Nicholas celebration to New Netherland. Maria Van Rensselaer purchased a variety of *Sinterklaesgoet* or Saint Nicholas goodies from local baker Wouter Albertsz vanden Uythoff (see page 13). These treats were ordered for the celebration in spite of the fact that the Reformed Church in New Netherland, whose principles were upheld by the West India Company, had outlawed the celebration of *Sinterklaas*. Similar prohibitions were imposed in the Netherlands too. Charles W. Jones in *Saint Nicholas of Myra, Bari, and Manhattan* notes an ordinance was issued in Amsterdam that meant "...to take the superstition and fables of the papacy out of the youths' heads. . . ." Historian Simon Schama has similar quotes of ordinances forbidding the celebration.

Descendants of the Dutch settlers continued to celebrate Saint Nicholas Day as their ethnic holiday well into the nineteenth century. This is clear from their hand-written cookbooks that date from the late seventeenth to the twentieth centuries. Most contain recipes for hard (*speculaas*) and soft gingerbread *(taaitaai)* or spiced honey cake (*zoete koek*, the cake from the town of Deventer). I have found almost forty such cookbooks, belonging to well-known Dutch families such as the Van Cortlandts of Croton-on-Hudson and New Amsterdam, the Van Rensselaers of Albany, the Lefferts of Brooklyn, and others.

Benevolent societies such as the Albany Saint Nicholas Society and later the New York Saint Nicholas Society also, held annual dinners on December 6. In the first fifty or so years of America's independence, holiday celebrations differed regionally. Most New England Protestants renounced religious holidays like Christmas in favor of secular holidays like Thanksgiving and New Year, while elsewhere others observed Christmas or Epiphany as their major holidays. For Dutch Americans, the celebration of Saint Nicholas as a feast for children continued and New Year's Day was the big social occasion for adults.

The transformation of Saint Nicholas into the uniquely American gift-giving figure we now know began, however, with the publication of Washington Irving's historical spoof *A History of New York* in 1809. Irving, himself of Scottish descent, but surrounded by Dutch neighbors and in-laws, describes Saint Nicholas riding the rooftops and ". . . drawing forth magnificent presents from his breeches pocket. . . ." Jones asserts "without Irving there would not be a Santa Claus." There was a precedent for a Father Christmas figure in Anglo-American culture, and in the melting pot way of this country, Santa Claus was an American adaptation of the beloved Dutch figure.

The word Santa Claus comes from the Dutch contraction *Sinterklaas*. I did not realize that apparently to American ears the Dutch word even sounds like it, as I discovered when I said *Sinterklaas* to someone and he thought I said "Santa Claus." Not only did Saint Nicholas's name change, but also his appearance: from a tall stern bishop he was transformed into a jolly, round, friendly santa smoking a Dutch clay pipe (these pipes were found by the dozens in archaeological excavations of Fort Orange, now Albany). In nineteenth-century American postcards and illustrations, we see many incarnations until today's Santa, who with his red outfit, black boots, belt, and long white beard, finally emerged by way of a 1930s Coca-Cola ad, which to me is so appropriately American. Clement Moore's poem *A Visit from Saint Nicholas,* the authorship of which is contested as I indicated before, published in 1823, added the reindeer. The poem might well have been written by Major Henry Livingston Jr. of Poughkeepsie (1748–1828), according to Dr. Charles Gehring, director of the New Netherland Research Center, who writes: "his descendants claim that he was the author but never took credit for it. Don Foster using computer technology makes a strong case in his book *Author Unknown: Tales of a Literary Detective* that the author was Livingston rather than Moore."

By 1866, illustrator Thomas Nast, building on the contemporary interest in arctic explorations, had created a home and workshop for Santa Claus at the North Pole. Gradually, the image and story we now know and love emerged.

The intertwined threads of the legend of Saint Nicholas can be followed from East to West and from Europe to the Americas. The tales about his numerous miracles linger through the centuries, but what has sustained his image most is his unselfish, anonymous giving, a quality that was transferred to his American counterpart when Saint Nicholas became Santa Claus.

Saint Nicholas arrives in Rotterdam by boat.

The Saint Nicholas Celebration in the Netherlands, United States, and Canada Today

WE CAN SAFELY SAY THAT THE *SINTERKLAAS* CELEBRATION is nowhere as popular as it is in the Netherlands. Belgium, which remained Catholic during the Eighty Years' War with Spain, also celebrates it but retains the Catholic character of a saint's day in a way that would not have been possible in the Protestant Netherlands. The Belgian celebration still takes place on December 6, whereas the Dutch celebrate their *Sinterklaasavond* on the night before. Since the Middle Ages, saint's days have been celebrated on the eve of their day.

In the Netherlands, as in America, a writer changed the way the Dutch presently celebrate Saint Nicholas Day. In 1850, school teacher Jan Schenkman wrote a very popular book, *Saint Nicholas and His Servant,* which for the first time, described Saint Nicholas as visiting families in person, rather than making imaginary rides over rooftops. Dressed as a Roman Catholic bishop, he was accompanied by a Moorish servant outfitted in a page costume, who would later get the name of *Zwarte* Piet or Black Pete, now so politically incorrect. (Usually friends or neighbors fill those roles.) The use of his name is now frequently debated in the Netherlands because of its implied racism. Much has been written about Black Pete's origin, and it seems most logical to me that he is based on sixteenth- or seventeenth-century pages as seen in the art of that period, though a book, *Zwarte Piet*, by Arno Langeler argues that he was the same historical figure, a Moorish war hero from Venice, that Shakespeare based his character Othello upon.

In 1839, Hildebrand, the pen name for writer, theologian, and minister Nicolaas Beets, published his *Camera Obscura* in which he looked at every day nineteenth-century life using his keen powers of observation and delicious sense of humor. One of his stories about a curious young man who attended a young women's *koek vergulden* (gilding of hard or soft molded gingerbread) party is still famous and often quoted during the *Sinterklaas* days. In it, the protagonist explains that gold leaf, a wet paint brush, and a soft brush, usually a rabbit's tail, are the tools needed to properly gild a cookie. And when he offers to help with this task, which was not considered a man's job, the women greet him with merriment. Correctly gilding a cookie takes patience, a steady hand, and quite a bit of skill to precisely follow the ridges of the mold, as my friend Debra Thimmesch can attest. She gilded and painted the large Saint Nicholas cookie (see page 37) more than 150 years after Hildebrand's story. For a while in the 1970s "gilding parties" became popular again, and today they are still held.

In the age of industrialization when Schenkman wrote his book, it seemed appropriate that Saint Nicholas would be a man of his time and arrive by steamboat from Spain.

But why Spain? Perhaps because the Dutch traded with Spain for fruits like oranges, but also because Saint Nicholas's remains were located in Bari, Italy, which during this time belonged to the Spanish empire. Modern day Dutch celebrations are still largely based on Schenkman's vision, though frequently *Sinterklaas* uses even more modern conveyances including a helicopter!

Throughout history, Saint Nicholas songs also played important roles. Besides commemorating the steamboat Saint Nicholas rode in, "See yonder comes the steamboat from Spain once again...," his songs were used as a way to communicate in wartime. During World War II a female prisoner sang some lyrics of Saint Nicholas songs—no doubt because every Dutch person knows them—to announce the passing and receiving of surreptitious messages.

Also during World War II, Anne Frank described in her diary how they celebrated *Sinterklaasavond* on December 7, 1942. First, everyone went downstairs to a dark, windowless room so they could turn on a light: "Daddy opened the big cupboard," she wrote, and "a large basket decorated with Saint Nicholas paper stood in the corner and on top there was a mask of Black Peter." The basket contained "a nice little present for everyone, with a suitable poem attached." The next year she and housemate Pim gave the gifts and stashed everyone's shoes that they had filled with little—no doubt homemade—presents in a laundry basket. Anne penned a heart-wrenching poem about their diminishing hopes, and yet maintained a spirit of festivity. (In August 1944, their hiding place was raided, and they were sent to German concentration camps, where Anne died of typhus.)

After World War II, the Dutch, whose affluence was growing, also started giving adults inventively wrapped presents and accompanying them with poems, while still maintaining an aura of mystery and anonymity as in the children's celebrations.

In order to understand how those of Dutch origin celebrate in other parts of the United States and Canada, we need to know their history. A second wave of Dutch immigration came to America in the mid-1800s, for religious reasons, and these Dutch settled in the states of Iowa, Wisconsin, and Michigan. And after World War II many Dutch emigrated to the Northwest and Canada.

The departure of three groups of Dutch to the United States in the 1840s had to do with *De Afscheiding* from the Protestant Church during that period. This schism, as well as dire economic circumstances, caused people to come to America looking for a better future, religious freedom, and education. The most important leaders were the ministers A. C. van Raalte from Arnhem, who departed from Dutch shores with his group in 1846, followed by H. P. Scholte from Utrecht and C. van der Meulen from Goes in the province of Zeeland, who both left in 1847. For (very) extensive information turn to Jacob van Hinte's *Netherlanders in America*; the nearly 1,200 fact-packed pages will tell you everything you want to know about this period of emigration and settlement.

As far as I have been able to ascertain, it was not until the 1970s that the Dutch descendants in Iowa and Michigan started to celebrate *Sinterklaas* with public events such as a Saint Nicholas parade and other festivities, based on the more modern Dutch holiday. However, since 1898, the Jaarsma bakery in Pella, Iowa, has been baking the specialties of the Dutch Saint Nicholas celebration, such as almond paste filled puff pastry letters and *speculaas.* The "letters" are renowned all over Iowa and now can be ordered together with other Dutch specialties by Internet from the Jaarsma website. I give a list of that and other mail order sources of Dutch products at the end of the book.

The latest wave of immigrants came after World War II and settled mostly in Canada. By May 1954, the one hundred thousandth Dutch immigrant had reached Canadian shores. Many had little or no money, but all had the will to work and make a better life for themselves. A wonderful book full of pictures documents their stories: *To All Our Children: The Story of the Postwar Dutch Immigration to Canada* by Albert VanderMey. The immigrants established themselves but still craved the tastes of the homeland. There are still various mail-order houses in Canada where you can order any Dutch product imaginable. (See resource guide)

Another way they kept current on all things Dutch was through two Dutch newspapers as well as a website www.dutchinamerica.com. One of the newspapers, *The Windmill Herald,* out of Langley, British Columbia, shut down in 2012. The other paper is the monthly *De Krant,* published in California, and it is still going strong. Recently its editor Tom Bijvoet launched a glossy bi-monthly publication called *Dutch, The Magazine.*

Like descendants of the early settlers, the later settlers also have not forgotten the taste of the foods of the homeland and continue to enjoy some of the Dutch specialties, particularly those served at holiday time, to this day. I hope this book will bring the Dutch in America tasty memories and give Americans a chance to get acquainted with our Dutch cooking and baking from the 111 recipes that follow, which span four centuries of Dutch treats.

Orange diamonds ***(Wener puntjes)***

Recipe on page 72

PART II

The Taste of December

Chewy *Taai-taai* cookies and mold

Recipe on page 27

Recipes for the Saint Nicholas (Sinterklaas) Celebration

ABC of spice mixtures *(Speculaaskruiden)*

Almond paste filled spiced cake (*Gevulde speculaas)*

Chewy honey cake (*Taai-taai)*

Coarse fondant (*Borstplaat)*

Holiday bread (*Duivekater)*

Letter cookies (*Koekletters)*

Marzipan figures *(Marsepein)*

Puff pastry letters filled with almond paste (*Banketletters)*

Small spiced cookies (*Pepernoten*)

Spiced cookies (*Speculaas)*

Spice nuts (*Kruidnoten)*

Thick hard gingerbread *(Speculaasbrok)*

THIS CHAPTER IS FILLED WITH RECIPES for some of the most special old and new *Sinterklaas* celebration treats. I hope you will make these a part of your holiday season. Before you begin baking the spiced cakes and cookies, you'll need to have traditional Dutch spice mixes on hand. So I am sharing with you three different mixtures of varying degrees of spiciness.

Some of the most popular treats are cakes and cookies that are made in molds. One of the oldest treats is *Taai-taai*, a chewy honey cake that is usually formed in wooden molds, but can also be cut into squares or diamonds. Another molded cake or cookie is a later version from the time when sugar became cheaper and more available. It is called *speculaas* from the Latin word *speculum* meaning mirror. Food historian William Woys Weaver suggests that the root word for *speculaas* comes from *specullus* or diminutive—harking back to small round molds used to imprint marzipan during the late Middle Ages. *Speculaas* cookies are now known in America as "windmill cookies" because they are most often baked in this shape.

Speculaas cookies are now known as "windmill cookies" in America.

Marzipan and molded sugar animal figures are also integral to *Sinterklaas*. My friend, professor Johanna Maria van Winter, believes the shapes were developed as a result of pre-Reformation church-imposed periods of fasting—such as Advent when *Sinterklaas* occurs. During fasting, the eating of four-footed animals and their products was forbidden, so creative bakers colored and shaped marzipan and coarse fondant to look like sausages, pigs, or cows (see page 12).

Letters were an early specialty as well. They originally were made of bread dough, then later of a richer cookie dough, shaped into alphabet forms, and baked. Finally, they were painted with a sugar glaze, and sometimes decorated with gold leaf or small comfits, which are candies consisting of fruit, seeds, or nuts coated in sugar. No matter what, they were an edible way of teaching children the alphabet. Nowadays, letters are made from rich puff pastry dough and filled with almond paste, or from cookie dough (see recipe, page 30). Chocolate factories now continue this tradition, making thousands of them every year out of milk, white or dark chocolate.

ABC *of spice mixtures (Speculaaskruiden)*

In the Netherlands, you can simply buy pre-made spice mixtures in the grocery store, but in the United States we have to make them ourselves. I think they are better and more flavorful when homemade. Here are three versions; you might choose not to use all of the mixtures in the recipes that follow, but you will need at least one, or you can have fun and try them all. Store spice mixtures in airtight containers in a dark place.

A. MILD

1 tablespoon ground cinnamon

½ teaspoon ground cloves

½ teaspoon ground mace

Scant ½ teaspoon ground ginger

¼ teaspoon ground cardamom

Combine all ingredients in a small bowl. Store in an airtight container in a dark place.

B. MEDIUM

4 teaspoons ground cinnamon

1 teaspoon freshly grated nutmeg

½ teaspoon ground anise seed

½ teaspoon ground ginger

¼ teaspoon finely ground white pepper

¼ teaspoon ground cardamom

¼ teaspoon ground coriander

¼ teaspoon ground cloves

Combine all ingredients in a small bowl. Store in an airtight container in a dark place.

C. SPICED

1 tablespoon ground cinnamon

½ teaspoon ground mace

½ teaspoon ground anise

½ teaspoon ground ginger

½ teaspoon ground cardamom

½ teaspoon freshly grated nutmeg

¼ teaspoon ground cloves

¼ teaspoon finely ground white pepper

¼ teaspoon finely textured salt

Combine all ingredients in a small bowl.
Store in an airtight container in a dark place.

Almond paste filled spice cake *(Gevulde speculaas)*

Almond paste filled spice cake (GEVULDE SPECULAAS)

I use mixture C for this cake recipe because it is more spiced than the commercially made version available in the Netherlands.

4 ounces almond paste, broken into small pieces
1 egg white
½ cup firmly packed dark brown sugar
1 tablespoon whole milk
1¼ cups all-purpose flour
8 tablespoons (1 stick) unsalted butter, softened, cut into pats
¼ teaspoon finely textured salt
¼ teaspoon baking powder
1 tablespoon spice mixture C
25 whole almonds

In an electric mixer, combine almond paste and egg white, and beat until smooth. Set aside.

Preheat oven to 350°F. In a large bowl, stir sugar and milk until sugar dissolves. Add flour, butter, salt, baking powder, and spice mixture. Combine and knead until a smooth dough forms. Divide in half. On a well-floured work surface, shape one half of the dough into a 10x5-inch rectangle. Use a rubber spatula to carefully spread almond paste mixture on dough. Roll out the second batch of dough into a 10x5-inch rectangle. With the help of a wide spatula place the second rectangle on top of the almond paste filling. Carefully press the sides down to cover the filling completely. This requires a bit of cut and paste work. With a sharp knife and a clean ruler, score the top into 25 (1x2-inch) pieces. Place a whole almond in the middle of each piece. Transfer to a buttered baking sheet. Bake on the middle shelf of the oven for 20 to 25 minutes until brown. Cool. To serve, cut into the pre-scored pieces. Yield: 25 pieces.

Chewy honey cake (TAAI-TAAI)

The Dutch name of this baked good, *Taai-taai,* means literally "toughtough," named for the cake's consistency, which is quite chewy. The recipe comes from a wonderful new Dutch baking book, *Het Nederlands Bakboek,* by Gaitri Pagrach-Chandra. We both agree that Dutch baked goods are exceptional. Her version for this centuries-old honey cake recipe is quicker to make than the original, which required the dough to rest for weeks, and creates a nice spiced and chewy product that keeps well. Note: Dough needs 1 hour chilling time. Parchment paper is needed for baking.

1 cup and 2 tablespoons rye flour

1 cup and 1 tablespoon all-purpose flour

1⅛ teaspoons baking soda

¾ teaspoon ground cinnamon

¾ teaspoon ground anise seed

¼ teaspoon ground ginger

⅛ teaspoon freshly grated nutmeg

⅓ cup honey

⅓ cup molasses

2 tablespoons water

1 egg, beaten

Sift two flours together with baking soda in a large bowl and stir in the spices. In a small saucepan combine the honey, molasses, and water. Warm it over low heat and slowly bring it to a boil. Stir frequently. As soon as small bubbles appear around the edges, turn off the heat and let the mixture cool to lukewarm. Pour into the dry ingredients and stir until a cohesive dough forms. Wrap in wax paper and refrigerate 1 hour. Transfer the dough to a floured work surface; dust lightly with flour and roll out with a floured rolling pin to a 8x12-inch rectangle. Cut with a sharp knife into sixteen 2x3-inch pieces. Brush with beaten egg and place on a baking sheet lined with parchment paper. Bake in a 400°F oven for 7 to 9 minutes. Transfer to a rack to cool. When cold, put the pieces in an airtight container and let stand for 24 hours for the flavors to marry, before eating. Yield: 16 pieces.

Coarse fondant (BORSTPLAAT)

This is a very typical treat for the *Sinterklaas* celebration. Fondant can be shaped into hearts or animals using metal cookie cutters, or if you have them, animal molds.

- 2 cups granulated sugar
- ½ cup water

Thoroughly butter small molds or open metal cookie cutters. Line a baking sheet with foil, and butter it thickly. Place the molds or cutters on the baking sheet. In a saucepan over low heat, combine sugar and water. Cover and cook until the sugar dissolves. In a small bowl, combine some water and ice cubes, and set aside. Uncover the saucepan, and stir sugar mixture until a drop of it, when allowed to fall from a spoon into the ice water bowl, forms a ball of chewing gum consistency, Then continue to stir the mixture until it becomes opaque. Remove from heat and quickly pour into molds or cookie cutters. Cool for about 30 minutes, then check to see if the tops have hardened. If so, then carefully set the molds upright to cool the other side. Remove from molds and store in an airtight container. Yield: depends on the size of molds used.

Holiday bread (DUIVEKATER)

The mysterious Dutch name for this bread, *Duivekater,* supposedly refers to both the devil and a tomcat, but it is not clear why. This bread purportedly represents a shinbone. It originated centuries ago as a bread offering at funerals. Note: Dough needs about 2 hours to rest and rise.

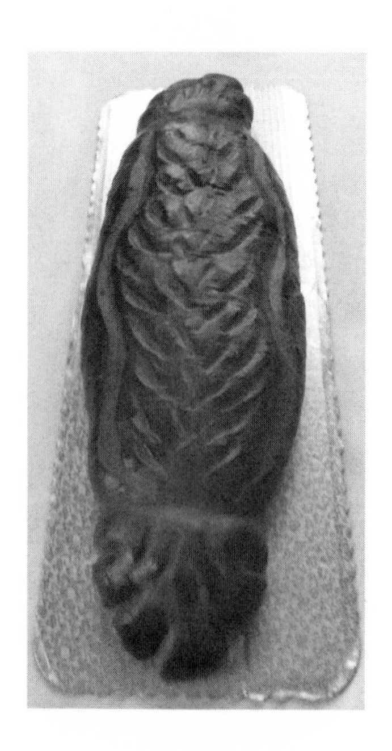

- ¼ cup lukewarm water (105°F to 115°F)
- 2 packages active dry yeast
- ½ teaspoon plus 1 cup granulated sugar, divided
- 4 cups all-purpose flour, or more as needed
- ¼ teaspoon finely textured salt
- 1 cup lukewarm whole milk (105°F to 115°F)
- 8 tablespoons (1 stick) unsalted butter, melted and cooled
- 1 teaspoon ground cinnamon
- 1 whole egg and 1 egg yolk, beaten
- 2 teaspoons finely grated lemon zest
- 1 egg beaten, for glazing the bread

Knead dough on a floured work surface.

Place warm water in a small bowl and sprinkle with yeast and the ½ teaspoon sugar. Stir and set aside. In a large bowl, sift flour and salt, and make a well in the middle. Once yeast has risen and is bubbly, pour it into the well with the milk and stir from the middle to incorporate both into the flour. Stir in butter, remaining sugar, cinnamon, egg, and yolk as well as the lemon zest. Knead the dough on a floured work surface for about 15 minutes; if sticky add more flour as needed. Note: This whole procedure can be done very successfully in an electric mixer, equipped with a dough hook, following manufacturer's instructions. Divide dough in half, cover with a moist towel, and allow to rise for 1 hour in a warm place. Remove and form into 2 pointed breads. Allow to rise again for another 45 minutes or so covered with a moist towel. Preheat oven to 350°F. If necessary, reshape the bread and cut the top of each in three parts and the bottom in two parts. Curl the outer parts on the bottom. Using a sharp knife or razor blade, cross-cut into the sides and top of each loaf a few times to make a decorative pattern. Brush the *Duivekaters* with the beaten egg and bake for 30 to 40 minutes, or until a toothpick inserted comes out clean. Cool on racks. Yield: 2 loaves.

Letter cookies (KOEKLETTERS)

These cookies are a good project to do with older children, age 8 and up. Before you make the recipe, you might want to practice together beforehand, using a piece of string to make the initial of the child's name and discuss the best and easiest way to do this using dough.

16 tablespoons (2 sticks) unsalted butter

½ teaspoon finely textured salt

1 cup confectioners' sugar

2 egg yolks

3 cups all-purpose flour

Preheat oven to 325°F. In an electric mixer, cream butter, salt, and sugar, add yolks, then flour in 4 batches. Beat to make a smooth, non-sticky dough that clings to the beater.

METHOD 1: Divide dough into 3 parts and work with 1 part at a time; refrigerate remaining dough. Roll dough out to about ½-inch thick and cut out with letter cookie cutters.

METHOD 2: This way is more fun to do with an older child. Divide dough into 3 parts and work with 1 part at a time; refrigerate remaining dough. Roll each part into an even rope, about ½ inch in diameter and 24 inches long, cut into 3 equal pieces. Roll each piece again and use to shape a letter. The dough is very easy to work with and very forgiving, just pat it into shape. Look at the illustration (see page 31) and try to decorate the letters in the way they appear there. Use a small knife to cut small grooves in the dough, horizontally and vertically, and give the ends a small cut in the middle and then curl each side outwards. Place on buttered baking sheets, and bake in batches for 20 to 30 minutes, until lightly browned. Cool on racks, and store in airtight containers. Yield: 9 letters, depending on size.

Letter cookies (*Koekletters*), unbaked

Letter cookies (*Koekletters*), baked. The cookies are decorated to resemble the letter cookies shown in seventeenth-century paintings.

Marzipan potatoes and carrots

Marzipan figures (MARSEPEIN)

Bakeries have a long history in the Netherlands. Because the country lacked forests, firewood for bake ovens was scarce and expensive. Therefore, rather than baking at home, most Dutch families relied on the local bakeries for breads, cookies, as well as holiday specialties, including marzipan.

Marzipan nut logs

By the middle of every November, Dutch bakeries are filled with *Sinterklaasgoed*—delicious edible items for the Saint Nicholas celebration, including pastries, chocolate, and marzipan figures. Marzipan is a mixture of almond paste, sugar, and egg whites. One historical thought on the origins of marzipan proposes that Arabians introduced sugar cane, sugar milling confectionery techniques, and the knowledge of making molded marzipan figures to Europe.

It had been my intention when I put together this chapter to give you instructions for making some appealing marzipan figures. On googling "marzipan figures," however, I found so many sources, and more importantly how-to videos, that I decided to not include my instructions as others have done a better job and given you easily accessible visuals to go along with them!

I want to share how to make three of the simplest versions of marzipan figures. The first is a marzipan "potato," which is a little ball of marzipan lightly dusted with cinnamon and cocoa powder. The second figure is a marzipan carrot. The third figure is a simple nut log. I serve these three together—the little potatoes, carrots, and nut logs—on *Sinterklaas* evening or for my yearly Christmas tea. They also could be part of the American Christmas cookie tray, of course. I use Danish Odense marzipan readily available in American supermarkets. I suggest you look at the company's website, www.odense.com, for many other wonderful and easy-to-make recipes.

Marzipan potatoes (AARDAPPELTJES)

1 teaspoon ground cinnamon

¼ teaspoon cocoa powder (I use Droste brand)

3½ ounces (half of a 7-ounce roll) marzipan (I use Odense brand)

Mix cinnamon and cocoa powder on a small plate and set aside. Roll marzipan into 14 balls, each the size of a marble. Quickly roll them in cinnamon mixture, but not enough to fully coat each ball. Roll again between your hands; this way you use just the right amount to cover the "potato" completely without getting too much coating. Yield: 14 potatoes.

Marzipan carrots

3½ ounces (half of a 7-ounce roll) marzipan (I use Odense brand)

Red and yellow food coloring

Fresh parsley sprigs, for decorating

Flatten the marzipan. Make a thumbprint in it, and put 2 drops each of red and yellow coloring into the center. Fold and re-fold until the orange color is evenly distributed. Cut the marzipan into 12 even pieces, and roll each piece into a small carrot shape. Use scissors to snip off ½-inch pieces of parsley stems without leaves and insert into the carrot top to resemble the trimmed off tops of carrot greens. With the blunt part of a knife, cut light grooves into the carrot to make it look even more realistic. Yield: 12 carrots.

Marzipan nut logs (MARSEPEIN MET WALNOOT)

7 ounces (1 roll) marzipan (I use Odense brand)

Colored or white granulated sugar

Whole walnuts halves

Cut the marzipan roll in half, and roll each half into a rope 1x4½-inches long. Roll each rope in sugar, and cut each rope into 6 (¾-inch) pieces. Push a walnut half on both ends. Repeat with remaining pieces. Yield: 12 logs.

Puff pastry letters filled with almond paste (BANKETLETTERS)

One of the most spectacular of the sweets for the Saint Nicholas celebration is a puff pastry filled with almond paste and shaped into the initial of the recipient or an S for *Sinterklaas,* which is one of the easiest letters to form. In America, the S could of course stand for Santa.

FOR THE PASTRY:

2 cups all-purpose flour

¼ teaspoon finely textured salt

1½ sticks cold unsalted butter, cut in half lengthwise, then cut into ¼-inch pieces

11 tablespoons ice water

1 egg plus 1 tablespoon water beaten, for egg wash

FOR THE FILLING:

10 ounces almond paste (not marzipan)

1 egg

TO MAKE THE PASTRY: Sift flour and salt into a bowl. Add butter to the flour. Add ice water to the mixture, and with a fork, stir dough until it barely holds together. Then, quickly press the dough with your hands until you can lift it from the bowl. Turn onto a lightly floured work surface. With a floured rolling pin, roll dough into a rectangle. This will be messy. Clean the rolling pin. Use a spatula to loosen the dough from the work surface. Fold the dough in thirds. Turn the dough. Roll again, fold, and turn. Repeat 4 or 5 times. The dough should be smooth without streaks of butter. Roll the dough into a long strip, about ⅛-inch thick, 24 inches long, and 5 inches wide. If the dough stretches back while you are rolling it, let it rest for a few minutes and it will be easier to handle.

TO MAKE THE FILLING: In an electric mixer, beat almond paste and egg until it becomes a smooth paste. Heavily flour your hands, and shape the paste into a 23-inch roll.

TO ASSEMBLE AND MAKE THE INITIALS: Place almond paste roll on the lower half of the pastry strip, leaving a ½-inch margin of dough on each side. Carefully brush the upper portion of the strip lengthwise with the egg wash. Roll the dough away from you, jelly-roll fashion, to enclose the almond paste. Make sure the seam is on the bottom, and seal the edges along the entire length. Fold the ends under and secure. You have now created a 24-inch filled rope, with which you can make any letter of the alphabet. Save the pastry scraps.

TO EXPERIMENT: Use a 24-inch piece of string and fashion the desired letter. This will help you understand where the connection will be made and how much to cut off for the piece that will be joined to form the letter.

TO MAKE THE LETTERS: Carefully place the rope onto an ungreased baking sheet that has been covered with ungreased foil, and shape into the chosen initial. Make sure the filled "rope" is not twisted, and the seam remains on the bottom.

The following letters require no cuts or inserts: C, G, I, J, L, M, N, S, U, V, W, and Z.

One cut and or one insert will be needed to form D, E, F, O, P, T, or Y. To make a D or O, open ends and press one together, moisten with egg wash, and insert into other end. Cut a ½-inch wide strip of scrap pastry, dip in egg wash, and neatly press over the insert to cover. Ease the pastry into the desired shape.

To form an E or F, cut off a small piece to form the center crossbar; seal one end of the cutoff piece and press the other end together. Moisten with egg wash. Shape the main portion of the pastry and cut a small slit to receive the crossbar; push the filling back and insert the pressed end. Cut a ½-inch strip of pastry, dip in egg wash, and use it to cover the seam. Shape the letter P and press the end together to be inserted. Moisten with egg wash, proceed as for E and F. To make a T, seal the ends of the crossbar. Cut a small slit in the middle and push back the filling. Seal one end of the stem, and press it together with the other end. Moisten with egg wash and insert in the slit in the crossbar. Proceed as for E and F. To make a Y, fashion a small U for the top portion of the letter and cut off the portion of the stem. Close the cut end. Cut a slit in the bottom of the U and push back the filling. Press together the cut end of the stem and moisten with egg wash and insert into the slit in the bottom of the U, proceed as in E and F.

Two cuts or inserts are required to make an A, B, H, R, X, or Q.

For A and H, shape the main part of the letter. Press together the ends of the crossbar. Moisten with egg wash. Cut two slits in the side bars and proceed as in E and F. To make a B, shape a P with a long stem up to meet the rounded portion of the P; this way only two inserts need to be made. Proceed with inserts as in E and F. The K is a difficult letter to shape, and experimenting with a piece of string will be useful. When you are satisfied with the proportions of your letter, cut a stem and two side bars. Insert one side bar in the middle of the stem, the other about one-third of the way up the side bar. Proceed with inserts as in E and F. To make an R, shape a P and cut one side bar. Insert the side bar into the rounded portion of the P. Proceed with inserts as in E and F. For an X, cut one long crossbar and two half size crossbars. Make two parallel slits in the middle of the long bar. Push the filling aside carefully and insert the two crossbar ends, which have been pressed together and moistened with egg wash. Proceed as in E and F. To make a Q, cut a small tail for the letter, then shape the main portion of the letter in an open O. Cut two parallel slits in the tail and insert the ends of the open O, which have been pressed together and moistened with egg wash. Proceed as in E and F.

TO FINISH AND BAKE THE LETTERS: Preheat oven to 400°F. Make sure all ends are sealed. Carefully brush entire pastry with egg wash. Bake one at a time for 30 minutes, or until golden brown. Cool on baking sheet. When cool, carefully peel off the foil, if necessary. This pastry is best made the day before it is to be served. To refresh or for leftovers, place in a 350°F oven for about 5 to 7 minutes.

Small spiced cookies (*Pepernoten*)

Small spiced cookies (PEPERNOTEN)

This recipe is adapted from the 1838 edition of the *Nieuw Nederlandsch Keukenboek* (*New Dutch Kitchenbook*). Most Dutch people will tell you that the minced citron is unusual, but they knew what they were doing back then, because it is a delicious addition. Citron (*Citrus medica*) is a citrus fruit. The candied rind is used here. Chopped candied citron is found on supermarket shelves together with other candied fruit during the holiday season.

1½ cups all-purpose flour
1½ cups granulated sugar
1 teaspoon ground cinnamon
1 teaspoon freshly grated nutmeg
1 teaspoon cardamom
1 teaspoon anise seed
1 tablespoon minced citron
3 eggs, beaten with a fork, divided

Preheat oven to 350°F. In a large bowl, combine flour, sugar, all spices, and citron. Add about half of the beaten eggs and knead to a stiff, but pliable dough. The eggs serve as the liquid in this recipe, therefore add more egg only 1 tablespoon at a time, so as not to make the dough too soft. Roll into balls the size of hazelnuts. Place on buttered baking sheets and bake in batches for about 15 minutes. Cool on racks, and store in airtight containers. Yield: 36 to 40 cookies.

Spiced cookies (SPECULAAS)

This is an essential cookie for the Dutch Saint Nicholas celebration. I like spice mixture C (see recipe page 25) but any will work.

1 tablespoon whole milk

⅓ cup packed dark brown sugar

6 tablespoons unsalted butter, softened

¼ teaspoon finely textured salt

1 cup all-purpose flour

1 tablespoon spice mixture A, B, or C

Toasted whole almonds

Preheat oven to 350°F. In a bowl, pour milk over sugar and stir to dissolve. In another bowl, thoroughly combine butter, salt, flour, and spice mixture. Stir in sugar mixture, and knead wet and dry ingredients until a smooth dough forms.

TO MAKE FLAT COOKIES: Shape into a 1¼x1¼-inch square log, and cut into ¼-inch thick squares. Arrange on lightly buttered baking sheets. Top each cookie with a whole almond.

TO MAKE MOLDED COOKIES: Oil, then flour a wooden mold, knocking out excess flour, and press dough into the mold. Cut off excess dough horizontally with a sharp knife. Turn the mold over on a lightly buttered baking sheet and tap it to release the molded images. If there is enough excess dough, gather it up, and repeat to make more.

Bake in batches for about 15 minutes, until light brown. Cool on racks, and store in airtight containers. Yield: 2 to 3 dozen cookies.

Debra Thimmesch gilding a large Saint Nicholas cookie.

The molded dough for the Saint Nicholas *speculaas* cookie, unbaked.
Note the mold in the background.

Debra Thimmesch's gilded Saint Nicholas *speculaas* cookie.

Spice nuts (KRUIDNOTEN)

This recipe uses the same spiced cookie dough. I use spice mixture C, but by using one of the other ones, you vary the cookies.

1 cup self-rising flour
4 tablespoons unsalted butter, softened
¼ teaspoon finely textured salt
¼ cup packed dark brown sugar
2 teaspoons molasses
2 teaspoons spice mixture A, B, or C
1 to 2 tablespoons water

Preheat oven to 350°F. In a food processor fitted with a metal blade, pulse flour, butter, salt, sugar, molasses, and spice mixture. With the machine running, add 1 tablespoon of water or 2, if necessary, to make a cohesive dough. Roll into marble-sized balls. Place on buttered baking sheets, and bake in batches for 20 minutes, until browned and done. Cool on racks, and store in airtight containers. Yield: 40 spice nuts.

Spice nuts (*Kruidnoten*)

Thick hard gingerbread (*Speculaasbrok*)

Thick hard gingerbread (SPECULAASBROK)

For variety, use different spice mixtures.

11 tablespoons unsalted butter, softened
¼ teaspoon finely textured salt
¾ cup packed dark brown sugar
2½ cups all-purpose flour
2 tablespoons spice mixture A, B, or C
½ teaspoon baking powder
¼ cup whole milk, or more as needed
Whole almonds

Preheat oven to 350°F. In an electric mixer, cream butter, salt, and sugar until thoroughly combined. Aadd flour, spices and baking powder and beat until combined. If the dough is too stiff, add milk 1 tablespoon at a time until dough is soft and pliable. On a floured work surface, roll dough into a 7x10-inch rectangle about ½-inch thick. Transfer the slab to a buttered baking sheet. Press almonds into dough at even distances. Place on the middle shelf in the oven, and bake for 30 minutes. Turn oven off, and leave the *Speculaasbrok* in for 10 more minutes, until brown and done. Yield: 1 large piece, which is broken or cut into smaller pieces as needed.

Christmas turban cake

Recipes for Christmas Treats

Almond paste filled puff pastry Christmas wreath (*Kerstkrans)*

Apple custard *(Appel vlade)*

Apple tart with anise in a cream crust (*Appeltaert met anijs)*

Braided herb bread letters *(Gevlochten broodletters)*

Candied quince squares *(Kweepeer koekjes)*

Christmas bread (*Kerstbrood)*

Christmas turban cake (*Kersttulband)*

Christmas wreath cookies (*Kerstkransjes)*

Cream horns with cream and crushed candy canes

Homemade chocolates

- chocolate, almond, and apricot clusters
- chocolate, granola, and walnut clusters
- chocolate and hazelnut clusters
- chocolate lollipops

Meringue wreaths (*Schuimkransjes)*

Pear tart *(Peren taert)*

Spiced sweet bread *(Zoete koek)*

Almond paste filled puff pastry Christmas wreath (KERSTKRANS)

This first recipe in this chapter is another bakery-made product in the Netherlands, but can be made at home with a bit of patience and care.

1 sheet homemade or frozen puff pastry, thawed (See recipe, page 34 or use Pepperidge Farm brand)

1 egg plus 1 tablespoon water beaten, for egg wash, or more as needed

12 ounces almond paste (not marzipan)

1 egg

⅓ cup red and green candied cherries

2 tablespoons apricot jam with 2 teaspoons water, for glazing

Preheat oven to 400°F.

PREPARE THE PASTRY: Either make the puff pastry by hand or purchase it commercially made. Frozen puff pastry usually comes in a package with 2 sheets, and for this recipe you will need only 1 sheet. Thaw according to package directions, then cut in half

Almond paste filled puff pastry Christmas wreath *(Kerstkrans)*

across. As you unfold the pastry it will stretch somewhat. Carefully place it on a lightly floured work surface, and unfold the other half. Brush egg wash in a ½-inch strip along the short sides of one of the sheets. Place the other half sheet on top of the moistened area to make a 24-inch long sheet. Roll lightly with a rolling pin to adhere the seam.

TO MAKE THE FILLING: In the bowl of an electric mixer or with a hand mixer, beat the almond paste and egg until it becomes a smooth paste. Quarter 3 tablespoons of candied cherries. Add to the paste and process briefly. Save remaining whole cherries to decorate the top. Tear off a 25-inch sheet of plastic wrap and place the almond paste on it. Heavily flour your hands and shape the paste into a 23-inch roll. Use the wrap to help you shape the roll.

TO ASSEMBLE AND MAKE THE WREATH: Place the almond paste roll on the lower half of the pastry strip, leaving a ½-inch margin of dough on each short side of the pastry sheet. Carefully brush the upper portion of the strip lengthwise with egg wash. Roll the dough away from you, jellyroll fashion, to enclose the almond paste. Make sure the seam is on the bottom, and seal the edges along the entire length. You have now created a 24-inch filled rope. Transfer to a buttered baking sheet. Brush one end of the rope with ½ inch of egg wash and carefully insert in the other end to make a ring. Press down to make sure the end is secured and closed. Brush the entire wreath with egg wash. Bake for 20 to 25 minutes or until golden. Turn off the oven and, allow to stand for 5 minutes. Place the baking sheet on a rack and cool the ring until lukewarm. In a small bowl, beat the apricot jam with water. Brush the apricot glaze over the entire wreath and decorate with whole red and green cherries. Yield: 1 wreath; 8 to 10 servings.

Apple Custard (APPEL VLADE)

The consistency of this custard is reminiscent of tapioca pudding, and has a lovely bright apple flavor. This recipe is another "oldie but goodie," and comes from the 1683 edition of *The Sensible Cook.*

2¼ pounds Golden Delicious apples

½ cup dry white wine

½ cup water

2 tablespoons salted butter

1 cup coarse fresh bread crumbs without crust, made from a good peasant-style white loaf

5 egg yolks

½ teaspoon ground ginger

2 to 4 tablespoons granulated sugar, to taste

Peel apples, quarter, and core. Cut each quarter in three slices lengthwise, then cut the slices across into small pieces. In a large saucepan over medium heat combine apple pieces, wine, water, and butter. Cook until apples are very soft, then mash. Stir in bread crumbs, mashing them as well. Whisk in egg yolks, ginger, and sugar. Reduce heat to low and continue cooking, stirring constantly, until custards thickens, about 3 to 4 minutes. Pour into a pretty bowl and serve at room temperature or chilled. Yield: 4 to 6 servings.

Apple tart with anise in a cream crust (APPELTAERT MET ANIJS)

Everyone enjoys the crust of this tart—made with heavy cream rather than butter—as much as the delicious filling. It is another recipe from *The Sensible Cook*. Note: The crust must be prepared in 2 batches. Note: currants, often called Zante currants, are small dried raisins and are found in supermarkets.

FOR THE CRUST:

4½ cups all-purpose flour, divided

1½ cups granulated sugar, divided

2 egg yolks, divided

2 cups heavy cream, divided

FOR THE FILLING:

6 (about 6 cups) Golden Delicious apples, peeled, cut into quarters, cored, and then cut across into slivers

⅓–¾ cup granulated sugar, depending on the sweetness of the apples

1 tablespoon ground cinnamon

1 cup currants

1½ teaspoons anise seed, crushed with a rolling pin, or whirled in the food processor

4 tablespoons salted butter, cut into pats

1 egg plus 1 tablespoon water beaten, for egg wash

MAKE THE CRUST: In a food processor fitted with a metal blade, combine 2¼ cups flour and ¾ cup sugar. Run the machine for a few seconds. Stir 1 egg yolk into 1 cup of cream, and with the machine running, pour egg cream into the flour mixture and process until a dough ball forms. Cover in plastic wrap and refrigerate. Make a second batch of dough using the remaining half of the ingredients.

ASSEMBLE THE FILLING: Preheat oven to 350°F. For the bottom crust, roll out one batch of dough into an 18-inch circle and fit into the bottom of a buttered 9- or 9½-inch springform pan, allowing the dough to overhang the pan by 1½ inches all around. Top with one-third of the apples. Combine the sugar and cinnamon, and sprinkle one-third of it over the apples. Next layer one-third of the currants, one-quarter of the anise seed, and one-third of the butter. Repeat layering of ingredients twice. For the top crust, roll out two-thirds of the second batch of dough into a 10-inch circle. Top the apple mixture with this second piece of dough, and tuck it in at the sides to completely cover the filling. Fold in the overhanging edge of the bottom crust and secure it to the top crust all around. Use a paring knife to cut out a zigzag pattern in the protruding rim. Roll out the remaining one-third of the second piece of dough and cut out a 1½x8-inch strip. Cut another zigzag edge on one long side of this piece. Cut out a 2½-inch circle out of the middle of the top crust of the pie and insert the strip of dough, curled into a tube, zigzag edge up. It will look like a crown and will form the "chimney" to release steam. Freeze the scraps for later use, or, if you wish, use them to make leaves and flowers to decorate the top crust. Moisten the bottom side of each decoration with a little water before placing on the crust. Brush the entire top with the beaten egg mixture and sprinkle with remaining anise seed.

BAKE THE TART: Place the pie on a baking sheet and bake for 1 hour and 20 minutes, or until the crust is golden and the apples are tender. This "taert" is especially good with ice cream or whipped cream. It is a beautiful, filling, and delicious dessert. Yield: 6 to 8 servings.

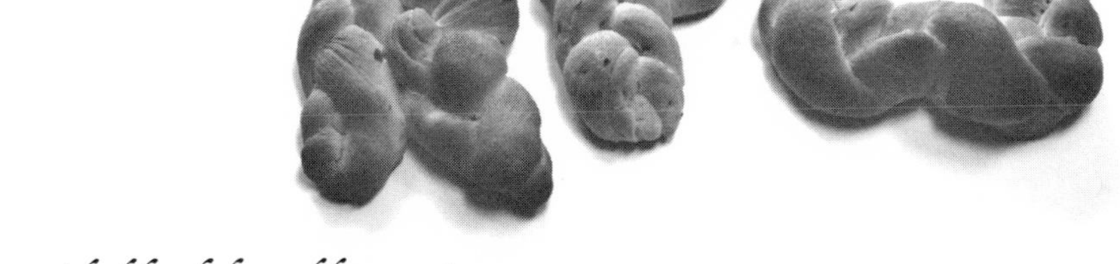

Braided herb bread letters (GEVLOCHTEN BROODLETTERS)

Use bread initials to indicate guests' places at your festive Christmas dinner or other December party. The letters serve a dual purpose of place marker and dinner roll. They are fun to make, and good to eat! Note: Dough needs about 2 hours to rest and rise.

3¼ cups all-purpose flour
1 teaspoon finely textured salt
2 packages rapid rise yeast
1 egg
⅔ cup whole milk, or more as needed, heated to 120°F to 130°F
8 tablespoons (1 stick) unsalted butter, melted
2 tablespoons scallions, minced
2 tablespoons parsley, leaves only, minced

Tablesetting with braided bread letter ***(Gevlochten broodletter)***

In an electric mixer, fitted with a dough hook, combine flour, salt, and yeast. Crack the egg into it and mix to combine. Pour in the milk and add the butter, scallions, and parsley. Beat the dough on the low setting for about 10 minutes, until the dough is smooth and elastic. You might find you need more milk, warm it first, then add to the dough. Grease a bowl, and place the dough ball in it, rolling it all around so all sides are greased. Move the dough to a warm, draft-free place, cover with a towel, and allow to rise for 45 minutes until it has almost doubled, turning the bowl occasionally so all sides stay warm.

Punch dough down, return it to the mixer and knead on the low setting for another 5 minutes. Transfer to a lightly floured work surface and cut into 12 equal pieces. Knead each piece into a smooth ball, and cut the balls each into 3 pieces. Roll each piece into a rope, then braid the 3 ropes and form the initial needed. Place on a buttered baking sheet and refine the forms as necessary. Let the letters rise in a warm, draft-free place for 30 to 40 minutes. Preheat oven to 450°F. After rising, reshape the initials again, as necessary. Bake the letters for about 15 minutes, or until light brown and done. Remove and cool on a rack. Yield: 12 initials.

Candied quince squares (KWEEPEER KOEKJES)

Like some of the previous recipes, this recipe comes from the definitive Dutch cookbook from the Golden Age, *De Verstandige Kok*, which I translated as *The Sensible Cook,* first published as part of a gardening book in 1667. I have tried all the recipes in the book, and they all work and are just wonderful. This quince candy with its pure fruit flavor is definitely worth the fuss! This often fuzzy-skinned fruit looks and tastes like a cross between a pear and an apple, and is available in U.S. supermarkets from September through December. Note: This recipe takes 3 or 4 days to complete drying, and you will need a kitchen scale.

2 large quince, quartered, peeled and cored

Granulated sugar

Red food coloring, if desired

DAY 1: In a small saucepan, place the quince pieces and completely cover them with water. Boil over medium-high heat until soft, about 25 minutes, until most of the water is evaporated. Drain thoroughly. (If desired, save the leftover cooking water and mix with a little sugar. This is delicious when added to applesauce.) Transfer to an airtight container and cool. Refrigerate overnight.

DAY 2: Remove the quince from the refrigerator, and place it on a clean work surface. Finely mash it with a fork. Weigh the quince paste. Then measure the same weight of sugar. Combine the two in a shallow saucepan and bring to a boil. Reduce heat and continue boiling while stirring constantly. At this point,1 or 2 drops of red food coloring may be added. Cook the quince until all liquid has evaporated, and the mass pulls away from the side of the pan, about 5 to 10 minutes. Cover a baking sheet with foil and sprinkle with a layer of sugar. Turn the cooked quince onto the sugar and shape into a neat rectangle. Preheat the oven to 250°F and place the baking sheet in the oven. Turn off the heat, and turn on the oven light. Leave in the oven overnight.

DAY 3 OR 4: In the morning check to see if the quince is dry on both sides. If not, turn it over on another sheet of sugar-covered foil and repeat placing the quince in a preheated oven overnight. The next day, when dry and not sticky on the outside, cut the rectangle into neat 1-inch squares. Store in an airtight container in a cool, dark place. Yield: about 3 dozen pieces.

Christmas bread (KERSTBROOD)

This recipe makes a wonderful bread for a festive Christmas breakfast, or just to have a slice with your coffee while the kids are opening their presents on Christmas morn. It can be made ahead and frozen, or kept for a few days before the big event in an airtight container.

3 packages active dry yeast
¼ cup warm water (100°F to 110°F)
Pinch granulated sugar
4½ cups plus 1 tablespoon all-purpose flour, divided
½ teaspoon finely textured salt
½ cup packed light brown sugar
½ cup whole milk, lukewarm
8 tablespoons (1 stick) unsalted butter, melted and cooled
2 egg yolks
1 cup raisins
1 cup currants (see note, page 46)
1 cup finely chopped candied fruit
1 cup slivered almonds
1 tablespoon lemon zest

Sprinkle the yeast over the warm water, then sprinkle the pinch of granulated sugar. Let stand 2 minutes and stir. Leave in a warm place until bubbly, about 5 minutes. In an electric mixer fitted with a dough hook, combine flour, salt, and brown sugar. Gradually mix in milk, melted butter, and egg yolks. Beat on the low setting for about 10 minutes, until the dough is smooth and elastic. If you need more milk, warm it first, then add it to the dough. Grease a bowl, and place the dough ball in it, rolling it all around so all sides are greased. Move the dough to a warm, draft-free place, cover with a towel, and allow to rise for 45 minutes until it has almost doubled, turning the bowl occasionally so all sides stay warm.

In a small saucepan, cover raisins and currants with water and bring to a boil. Turn off the heat and let stand for 5 minutes. Drain and dry thoroughly and mix with 1 tablespoon of flour.

When ready, turn out dough onto a floured work surface and knead in the prepared raisins, currants, candied fruit, slivered almonds, and lemon zest. Place dough in a long (12x4½x2½-inch-deep) loaf pan and cover with a towel. Set in a warm place to rise again for 45 minutes. Preheat oven to 400°F. Bake for about 30 minutes, or until a toothpick inserted comes out clean. Yield: 1 loaf.

Christmas turban cake (KERSTTULBAND)

Traditionally, the little cupcake in the middle of the turban cake is for the youngest child in the family, or the youngest person present. Note: I use a disposable 6-cavity foil cupcake pan and cut off all but 2 cups. Don't use a mini muffin pan. The cupcake needs to be big enough, but not too small, to fit comfortably in the center of the bundt cake. The extra cupcake is a bonus for the baker!

1 cup raisins

1 cup currants (see note, page 46)

1 cup minced candied fruit

1 cup minced candied ginger

3 tablespoons plus 5 cups cake flour, divided use

1 pound (4 sticks) unsalted butter, plus extra for buttering the pans

1 teaspoon finely textured salt

2⅔ cups granulated sugar

10 eggs, room temperature

3 tablespoons brandy

Confectioners' sugar, for topping

Undecorated turban cake.
Decorated turban cake, page 42.

Thoroughly butter a 9½-inch bundt pan and a disposable cupcake pan. Set aside.

Place raisins and currants in a small saucepan and cover with water. Bring to a boil and simmer for 5 minutes. Drain thoroughly and pat *completely dry* with paper towels. Mix with candied fruit and ginger, and toss with 3 tablespoons of cake flour. Set aside. Preheat oven to 350°F. In an electric mixer fitted with a cake beater or whisk beat butter, salt, and sugar at medium speed for about 5 minutes until fluffy and almost white. Add eggs one at a time and incorporate each one completely before adding the next. Add brandy and combine. Sift in flour by hand. Then using a spatula in an under-over motion, gently combine flour and fruit mixture into batter. Spoon into the prepared pan, and bake for about 1 to 1½ hours, or until a toothpick inserted comes out clean. Bake the little cakes alongside and remove after approximately 30 minutes, or until a toothpick inserted comes out clean. Cool cakes on a rack. Place the large cake on a platter and place the little cake in the hole of the big cake. Sift confectioners' sugar over both. Yield: 1 bundt cake, 2 cupcakes; at least 12 servings. (Thinner slices actually taste better.)

Christmas wreaths (KERSTKRANSJES)

Some years, I tie a thin red ribbon on these cookies and hang them on my Christmas tree. (Not a good idea if you have pets!)

2 cups all-purpose flour

12 tablespoons (1½ sticks) unsalted butter, room temperature

¼ teaspoon finely textured salt

¾ cup packed light brown sugar

1 tablespoon grated lemon zest

1 egg, beaten with a fork, divided

Sliced almonds

Preheat oven to 350°F. In a food processor, combine flour, butter, salt, sugar, zest and 2 tablespoons of the beaten egg and process until it forms a ball. On a lightly floured work surface, roll out the dough to approximately ⅜-inch thick and cut out 18 cookies with a round (3-inch) cutter, if you have one, or cut out rounds with a thin-rimmed glass dipped in flour. Then using a small round (about 1-inch) cutter or a small floured glass, cut out the center of each cookie to create the wreath shape. (Don't throw away the little center circles of dough. Top them with a few sliced almonds or chocolate chips and bake them separately.) Brush each cookie with the remainder of the beaten egg and sprinkle with the thin almond slices. Place on a buttered baking sheet and bake for 15 minutes, or until light golden. Transfer to a rack and cool. Yield: 18 (3-inch) cookies.

Christmas wreaths *(Kerstkransjes)*

Cream horns with cream and crushed candy canes

Cream horns with cream and crushed candy canes

Cream horns are found in every Dutch bakery shop, but this is my American twist—adding crushed candy canes to the cream filling to make a festive Christmas pastry. Note: You will need 6 cream horn molds (see resource guide or available on amazon.com)

- **1 sheet frozen puff pastry, thawed (I use Pepperidge Farm brand)**
- **1 egg, beaten lightly with a fork, for egg wash**
- **½ pint heavy cream**
- **2 tablespoons granulated sugar**
- **2 or 3 candy canes, crushed into small pieces**

MAKE THE HORNS: Heavily butter the outside of the cream horn molds and set aside. Preheat oven to 400°F. Unfold the pastry sheet and cut it into 6 (1x9½-inch) pieces. Take one strip at a time and carefully fold it over the mold with edges overlapping, forming a cone. Cut off any excess, and repeat with remaining molds. Brush horns with egg wash and place on a buttered baking sheet. Bake for 12 to 15 minutes, or until golden brown. Remove to racks, cool, and remove from molds.

MAKE THE FILLING: In an electric mixer, whip the cream with the sugar and stir in the crushed candy canes. Fill the horns with the cream mixture and serve. Yield: 6 horns. Note: The pastry scraps can be made into a kind of snickerdoodles. Gather all the excess dough, roll them into a ball, and pat flat. Spread with some butter and heavily sprinkle with cinnamon sugar—1 tablespoon sugar mixed with 1 teaspoon ground cinnamon. Roll in jellyroll fashion and cut into ½-inch rounds. Bake along side the horns and remove when browned.)

Homemade chocolates

Some thirty years ago, I wrote a little book on chocolate, *Festive Chocolate*, which is out of print but used copies are available on the Internet. I had a lot of fun creating new recipes for candies that could be either party favors or part of the holiday cookie tray. I have never given up this love for playing with chocolate. For Christmas I often use cellophane bags tied with red and gold ribbon to make goodie bags filled with homemade chocolates as presents for friends and family. Now, thirty years later, chocolate has become the rage in America and in Europe. The chocolate shop of Pierre Marcolini in Brussels even calls itself a "Haute Chocolaterie," equating it to haute couture or haute cuisine!

The first three recipes are very simple and require only stirring. The fourth recipe for lollipops is even easier! When I created the chocolate, almond, and apricot clusters, I was immediately hooked. Once you make them, you'll want to try your own combinations. Note: When working with chocolate, be extra careful so you don't ruin it. Chocolate can "seize"—meaning it can become granular and separate (which you don't want)—if it is cooked too long or at too high a temperature.

Chocolate, almond, and apricot clusters

Chocolate, almond, and apricot clusters

1 cup whole almonds

8 ounces semisweet chocolate chips

½ cup dried apricots, cut into half lengthwise and then each half into 3 pieces

3 dried apricots, cut into small pieces for topping

Preheat oven to 300°F. Spread almonds in a single layer in a shallow pan and toast for about 15 minutes, stirring once. Cool. Melt chocolate in a shallow bowl in the microwave. Start with 1 minute, remove, and stir; repeat for 20 seconds, then 10 seconds at a time, until completely melted. Carefully remove bowl from the microwave. Stir in the cooled almonds and apricot pieces. Drop by heaping teaspoons onto baking sheets covered with foil. For extra decoration, top each cluster with a small apricot piece. Refrigerate until cool and hardened. Store refrigerated in airtight containers. Yield: 22 to 24 clusters.

Chocolate, granola, and walnut clusters

8 ounces semisweet chocolate chips

1 cup granola (your favorite kind)

½ cup mixed black and golden raisins

½ cup chopped walnuts

Melt chocolate in a shallow bowl in the microwave. Start with 1 minute, remove, and stir; repeat for 20 seconds, then 10 seconds at a time, until completely melted. Carefully remove bowl from the microwave. Stir in granola, raisins, and walnuts. Drop by heaping teaspoons onto baking sheets covered with foil. Refrigerate until cool and hardened. Store refrigerated in airtight containers. Yield: 22 to 24 clusters.

Chocolate and hazelnut clusters

8 ounces semisweet chocolate chips

½ cup hazelnut spread (I use Nutella brand)

1 cup chopped hazelnuts

24 whole hazelnuts

Melt chocolate in a shallow bowl in the microwave. Start with 1 minute, remove, and stir; repeat for 20 seconds, then 10 seconds at a time, until completely melted. Carefully remove bowl from the microwave. Stir in the hazelnut spread and chopped hazelnuts. Drop by heaping teaspoons onto baking sheets covered with foil and top each with a whole hazelnut. Refrigerate until cool and hardened. Store refrigerated in airtight containers. Yield: 22 to 24 clusters.

Chocolate lollipops

Chocolate lollipops

These are so incredibly easy to make you will be amazed. For Christmas, I like the combination of the chocolate and crushed candy canes, but the fruit mixture works too. Note: You will need 6 wooden sticks that look like small tongue depressors (available at craft stores). Needs at least 4 hours to chill.

8 ounces semisweet chocolate chips

4 tablespoons crushed candy canes OR a combination of the following three:

2 tablespoons chopped pecans or walnuts

2 tablespoons slivered almonds

2 tablespoons golden raisins or dried cranberries

Sea salt, optional

Cover a baking sheet with foil and set aside. Melt chocolate in a shallow bowl in the microwave. Start with 30 seconds, remove, and stir; repeat for 20 seconds, then 10 seconds at a time, until completely melted. Carefully remove bowl from the microwave and scoop 6 circles of chocolate onto the foil-covered baking sheet. Push a wooden stick or tongue depressor high into the chocolate, and if necessary, scoop a little more chocolate on top to make sure the stick will hold the lollipop. Top each with either just the crushed candy canes, or a mixture of nuts, raisins or cranberries. Add a sprinkling of sea salt, if desired. Refrigerate for at least 4 hours. Remove from wax paper and carefully wrap each lollipop in plastic wrap and secure with a twist tie or a little ribbon. After you have made these once, you will come up with your own delicious topping combinations. Yield: 6 lollipops.

Meringue wreaths (SCHUIMKRANSJES)

You can tie a thin red ribbon around the meringue wreaths and hang them on your Christmas tree, or combine them with a sprig of evergreen and use them by each place setting at your holiday table. Leave the rest for the cookie tray! Note: You'll need a pastry bag and a star-shaped tip.

2 egg whites

1 cup granulated sugar

Red or green food coloring, if desired

Preheat oven to 300°F. In an electric mixer, beat egg whites until very stiff peaks form. Add sugar 1 tablespoon at a time. For red or green wreaths add food coloring and mix to the right color, if desired. When all of the sugar is completely incorporated, spoon the mixture into a pastry bag fitted with a star-shaped tip. Line a baking sheet with parchment, and pipe on circles until all the meringue is used. Place the baking sheet in the oven and reduce the temperature to 250°F. Bake for 1 hour. When done enough, they are easily removed from the paper. Store in airtight containers. Yield: 24 wreaths.

Meringue wreaths *(Schuimkransjes)*

Pear Tart (PEREN TAERT)

This lovely recipe, like the candied quince squares, comes from *The Sensible Cook.* It is not difficult to make and just delicious!

FOR THE CRUST:

2 cups all-purpose flour

⅓ cup packed light brown sugar

11 tablespoons cold unsalted butter, cut into pats

¼ teaspoon finely textured salt

2 egg yolks, lightly beaten with a fork

1 teaspoon rose water (OK to omit or purchase online at amazon.com)

FOR THE FILLING:

1 cup currants (see note, page 46)

6 large pears (about 1½ pounds), ripe but not mushy, peeled, cored, cut into quarters and then into 2 or 3 lengthwise slices (if very large, cut the slices in half crosswise as well)

⅓–½ cup granulated sugar, depending on the sweetness of the pears

½ teaspoon dried ground ginger

1 teaspoon ground cinnamon

MAKE THE CRUST: Lightly butter a 9-inch springform pan. In a food processor fitted with a metal blade, combine flour, sugar, butter, salt, egg yolks, and rose water, if desired. Process just until a cohesive dough forms. Press the dough on the bottom and 1¼ inch up on the sides of the prepared pan. Run your thumb around the rim to even it.

MAKE THE FILLING: Preheat oven to 350°F. Place currants in a small saucepan and cover with water. Boil 1 minute, remove from heat, and let stand 5 minutes. Drain and dry currants completely. and combine them with pear slices, sugar, and spices. Spread the filling evenly in the crust. Bake for about 50 to 60 minutes, until the crust is golden and the pears are tender. Yield: 8 to 10 servings.

Spiced Sweet Bread (ZOETE KOEK)

This is my adaptation of an age-old recipe. The town of Deventer in the Netherlands has been famous for this kind of gingerbread for centuries. Anne Van Cortlandt-Stevenson (1774–1821), who lived in Croton-on-Hudson, New York, recorded a recipe called "Honey Cooke" that is closely reminiscent of this cake, and demonstrates the longevity and popularity of traditional Dutch recipes. A slice of this cake, with or without butter and a cup of coffee, would be a nice and easy way to begin Christmas morning when there are packages to be opened and gifts to be admired. It is also a good sweet bread to bring to a church coffee-hour.

2 cups all-purpose flour
1 teaspoon baking powder
1 teaspoon ground cinnamon
½ teaspoon freshly grated nutmeg
½ teaspoon ground cloves
1 cup packed dark brown sugar
1 cup whole milk

Preheat oven to 350°F. In a large bowl, sift flour and spices, add brown sugar and combine. Slowly add milk and stir until a smooth dough forms. Spoon into a buttered 1.5 quart or 8½x4½x3-inch loaf pan, and bake for about 1 hour, or until a knife inserted comes out clean, and the loaf is a deep brown. Cool on a rack. This is a dense loaf that keeps well and improves in flavor and texture when stored in an airtight container for a few days. Yield: 8 servings.

6

Recipes for Today's American Cookie Tray

Almond paste cookies (*Weesper moppen*)

Anise cookies (*Friese duimpjes*)

Bar cookies with cinnamon and shaved almonds (*Jan Hagel*)

Caraway cookies (*Karwijzaad koekjes*)

Chewy lace cookies (*Kletskoppen*)

Chocolate almond crunchies

Chocolate orange swirls (*Chocolade-en sinaasappelkrullen*)

Coconut jam squares (*Kokoskoekjes*)

Currant cookies (*Krentenkoekjes*)

Ginger cookies (*Gemberkoekjes*)

Hazelnut triangles (*Hazelnootkoekjes*)

King's cookies (*Koningskoekjes*)

Meringue sticks dipped in chocolate (*Bokkepootjes*)

Orange diamonds (*Wener puntjes*)

Sugared puff pastry ovals (*Arnhemse meisjes*)

Tea *cookjes (Thee koekjes)*

Almond Paste Cookies *(Weesper Moppen)*

Almond paste cookies (WEESPER MOPPEN)

These cookies have a slightly chewy center. In Dutch, *Weesper Moppen* means "bricks or chunks from Weesp," which is a small town east of Amsterdam on the Vecht River and is famous for its almond paste cookies.

8 ounces almond paste

½ cup granulated sugar, divided

½ teaspoon grated lemon zest

1 large egg, beaten with a fork (you will only use half)

Preheat oven to 350°F. In an electric mixer cream the almond paste with ¼ cup sugar, zest, and 1½ tablespoon egg. Divide dough in half. Take 2 sheets of wax paper and on each sheet sprinkle ⅛ cup of sugar. Place one dough ball on each sheet, and roll each piece of dough into an 8-inch log covered with sugar. Freeze the logs, wrapped in the paper, for 30 minutes. On a cutting board cut each log into 14 slices with a sharp knife held at a 45-degree angle, arrange the slices 1 inch apart on lightly buttered baking sheets, and bake them in batches in the middle of the oven for 18-20 minutes, or until they are pale golden. Cool on racks, and store in airtight container. Yield: 28 cookies.

Anise cookies (FRIESE DUIMPJES)

The northern province of Friesland is particularly known for their anise-flavored, thumb-sized morsels. Every village or town bakery seems to have a slightly different version.

11 tablespoons unsalted butter
¼ teaspoon finely textured salt
1 cup packed dark brown sugar
1 egg
1 teaspoon ground cinnamon
½ teaspoon ground ginger
1 teaspoon crushed anise seeds
2¼ cups all-purpose flour

Preheat oven to 350°F. In an electric mixer, cream butter, salt, sugar, and egg. Add spices and flour. Keep beating until a cohesive dough forms. Divide into 3 pieces, and on a floured work surface, roll each into 10-inch long logs. Then flatten the logs until they are 2 inches wide and ½-inch thick. With a knife, cut lightly into the top of each flattened log to create a decorative crisscross pattern. Wrap each rectangle in wax paper and refrigerate for 30 minutes. Remove and cut rectangles into ½-inch, thumb-sized cookies. Arrange on lightly buttered baking sheets about 1-inch apart. Bake in batches for 18 to 20 minutes. Cool on racks, and store in an airtight container. Yield: 5 dozen cookies.

Bar cookies with cinnamon and shaved almonds (JAN HAGEL)

In 1991, I collaborated with Dutch master baker Peter de Jong for an article on Dutch cookies for *Gourmet* magazine. Nearly 20 years later *Gourmet* published *The Gourmet Cookie Book: The Single Best Recipe from Each Year, 1941–2009,* and they featured these bar cookies with cinnamon and shaved almonds for their single best recipe of 1991.

14 tablespoons unsalted butter, softened
¼ teaspoon finely textured salt
½ cup packed light brown sugar
1 teaspoon grated lemon zest
1 egg, lightly beaten with a fork, divided
2¼ cups all-purpose flour
½ cup sliced almonds
2 tablespoons granulated sugar
1 teaspoon ground cinnamon

Preheat oven to 350°F. In an electric mixer, cream butter, salt, sugar, zest, and half of the beaten egg until light and fluffy. Stir in flour. Place dough on a buttered baking sheet with a rim and flatten into a 10x14-inch rectangle. Brush with the rest of the egg, and cover with almonds. Combine sugar and cinnamon, and sprinkle neatly over almonds. Bake for 22 to 25 minutes, or until golden. Remove and cut immediately into 1x2-inch rectangular pieces. Cool on racks, and store in airtight containers. Yield: About 48 small bars.

Caraway cookies (KARWIJZAAD KOEKJES)

This easy drop cookie is adapted from the hand-written cookbook belonging to Anna de Peyster (1701–1774). She suggests: "drop them in lumps as big as nutmegs." She was the maternal aunt of Pierre Van Cortlandt of Croton-on-Hudson. Van Cortlandt Manor is now a historic museum, administered by Historic Hudson Valley.

½ cup unsalted butter
¼ teaspoon finely textured salt
1 cup granulated sugar
2 eggs
1 tablespoon caraway seed, crushed with a rolling pin
2 cups all-purpose flour

Preheat oven to 350°F. In an electric mixer, fitted with a flat beater, cream butter, salt, and sugar. Add eggs one at a time and combine thoroughly. Add caraway and flour a little at a time and combine. Use two small spoons to shape the cookies about the size of a nutmeg. Arrange balls on buttered baking sheets about 1½ inches apart, and bake in batches for about 15 minutes, or until light brown. Cool on racks, and store in airtight containers. Yield: 4 dozen cookies.

Chewy lace cookies (KLETSKOPPEN)

The Dutch name *kletskoppen* means "pat-on-the-heads." It might be necessary to tap the cookies while they bake to help them spread. They are slightly chewy in the middle and crisp on the outside with a butterscotch-like taste.

¾ cup all-purpose flour
½ teaspoon ground cinnamon
Pinch finely textured salt
4 tablespoons unsalted butter, softened
¾ cup packed dark brown sugar
½ cup finely chopped almonds
1 tablespoon water

Preheat oven to 400°F. In a food processor fitted with a metal blade, pulse all ingredients until a cohesive dough forms. Roll dough into small balls about the size of large marbles. Arrange them on buttered baking sheets about 2 inches apart. Place on the highest shelf in the oven, and bake in batches for 6 to 8 minutes, until light brown (check after 5 minutes, and if necessary tap with the back of a wooden spoon to help them spread). Do not overbake as they will turn bitter. Cool on racks, and store in airtight containers. Yield: 36 cookies.

Chocolate almond crunchies

This recipe was given to me by Harriet B. Risley for a little chocolate book I wrote in 1986, now long out of print. The recipe remained, however, and is an all-time favorite in my family (and not only at holiday time). I bake the cookies and then sit down and watch a bit of television while I roll the still warm cookies in the sugar/cacao/cinnamon mixture. It makes a crunchy, satisfying small morsel. Not too much, not too little, it is just right to still that momentary chocolate craving.

½ cup unsalted butter, softened
¼ teaspoon finely textured salt
1 tablespoon packed light brown sugar
2 tablespoons granulated sugar
1 cup all-purpose flour
½ teaspoon pure vanilla extract
½ cup toasted almonds, chopped
½ cup miniature semisweet chocolate chips

SUGAR MIXTURE FOR COATING:

½ teaspoon ground cinnamon

1 cup confectioners' sugar

1 heaping teaspoon cocoa powder (I use Droste brand; available on amazon.com)

Preheat oven to 350°F. In an electric mixer, cream butter, salt, and sugars, add flour, vanilla, and almonds and combine. Stir in chocolate chips. Roll dough into 1-inch balls. Place on buttered baking sheets, and bake in batches for about 15 minutes. In a small bowl, combine the cinnamon, sugar, and cocoa powder. Remove cookies from oven and while still warm, roll in cinnamon mixture. Cool on racks, and store in airtight containers. Yield: 3 dozen cookies.

Chocolate orange swirls (CHOCOLADE–EN SINAASAPPELKRULLEN)

This recipe is another result of my collaboration with Dutch master baker Peter de Jong. These rich cookies are testimony to the harmonious marriage of chocolate and orange, and they are a beautiful addition to the American cookie tray.

1 cup (2 sticks) unsalted butter, softened

½ teaspoon finely textured salt

1 cup granulated sugar

2 cups all-purpose flour

2 teaspoons freshly grated orange zest

1 tablespoon unsweetened cocoa powder (I use Droste brand; available on amazon.com)

Preheat oven to 350°F. In an electric mixer, cream butter, salt, and sugar, add flour, and continue beating until a cohesive dough forms. Transfer half the dough to a small bowl and stir in zest. In another bowl, combine the remaining dough and cocoa powder. Between 2 sheets of wax paper roll orange dough into a 12x7-inch rectangle. Remove the top sheet. Between 2 more sheets of wax paper roll chocolate dough into an 11x6-inch rectangle. Remove the top sheet, and invert the chocolate dough onto the orange dough. Remove the top sheet of paper. Using the bottom sheet as a guide and with the long side facing you, roll doughs together, jellyroll fashion. Wrap the log in wax paper and chill for 45 minutes. On a lightly floured surface, roll the log until it measures 13½ inches long. Cut it crosswise into rounds ¼-inch thick, and arrange them 1-inch apart on lightly buttered baking sheets. Bake in batches on the middle shelf of the oven for 18 minutes or until they are pale golden. Cool on racks, and store in airtight containers. Yield: about 50 cookies.

Coconut jam squares (KOKOSKOEKJES)

Here is a wonderful bar cookie recipe that is easy to make. You cannot have enough of those sorts of recipes.

1¾ cups all-purpose flour

1 stick plus 3 tablespoons unsalted butter, cold, cut into pats

¼ teaspoon finely textured salt

1 cup loosely packed light brown sugar

5 tablespoons raspberry or apricot jam

3 egg whites

Grated zest of 1 lemon

7 ounces sweetened coconut

Preheat oven to 350°F. In a food processor fitted with a metal blade, pulse flour, butter, salt, and sugar, until a cohesive dough forms. Transfer to a buttered baking sheet with rim and with a floured rolling pin roll out to a 10x10-inch square, ¼-inch thick. In a small bowl, place 5 tablespoons of jam and stir with 1 tablespoon of water (or a little more as necessary). With a pastry brush neatly brush the top of the dough piece with jam to cover. In an electric mixer beat the egg whites until stiff. Gradually add zest and coconut until combined. Brush this mixture on top of the jam layer. Bake for about 30 minutes, then while still hot, cut into 2x2-inch bars. Cool on racks, and store in airtight containers. Yield: 25 squares.

Currant cookies (KRENTENKOEKJES)

This recipe is for one of my favorite cookies because it is crunchy and chewy at the same time and very easy to make!

1½ cups unsalted butter, softened

½ teaspoon finely textured salt

1 cup packed dark brown sugar

3 cups all-purpose flour

1 cup currants (see note, page 46)

Preheat oven to 350°F. In an electric mixer, cream butter, salt, and sugar; add flour a little at a time. Stir in currants. Roll dough into 1-inch balls, and arrange them on buttered baking sheets, about 2 inches apart. Press down on each ball with a fork to make a crisscross pattern, or flatten with the bottom of a floured glass. Bake for 15 to 18 minutes. Cool on racks, and store in airtight containers. Yield: 3 dozen cookies.

Ginger cookies (GEMBERKOEKJES)

In the Netherlands, ginger is usually sold in a jar with syrup, and so for this recipe, you would drain and chop those pieces. Since crystallized ginger is more readily available in the United States, I use it in the ginger cookies instead, and it works quite well. Dutch home cooks use self-rising flour more often than their American counterparts do. It makes quick work of baking these cookies, and the dough can also be made a day ahead and refrigerated until ready to use. On top of that, this is a terrific little cookie, if you like ginger!

1 cup self-rising flour

⅓ cup plus 2 tablespoons granulated sugar, divided

¼ teaspoon finely textured salt

8 tablespoons unsalted room-temperature butter, cut into pats

4 tablespoons packed finely chopped crystalized ginger

In a food processor fitted with a metal blade, pulse flour, ⅓ cup of sugar, salt, and butter until a cohesive dough forms. Mix in ginger. Transfer to a lightly floured work surface and roll into a long log about 1½ inches in diameter. Sprinkle the remaining 2 tablespoons of sugar on the work surface and roll the log in sugar, coating it completely. Cover in plastic wrap, and refrigerate for 30 minutes. Preheat oven to 350°F. Cut the roll into ¼-inch thick slices and arrange on buttered baking sheets. Bake for 15 minutes, or until light brown. Cool on racks, and store in airtight containers. Yield: 24 to 25 cookies

Hazelnut triangles (HAZELNOOTKOEKJES)

Hazelnuts are a favorite nut in the Netherlands. In this recipe, I use them in a sweet cookie, and in chapter 7, I pair them with Old Amsterdam cheese to make savory cookies (see recipe, page 90).

½ cup butter, unsalted softened

¼ teaspoon finely textured salt

⅓ cup packed dark brown sugar

1 cup all-purpose flour

½ cup finely chopped hazelnuts

36 halved hazelnuts

Preheat oven to 350°F. In an electric mixer, cream butter, salt, and sugar; add flour a little at a time, and add in chopped hazelnuts. Transfer the dough to a lightly floured surface and roll it into a log 10 inches long. Now the objective here is to shape the round log into a 3-dimensional, triangular-shaped log. First press down just enough on the top of the log to flatten the bottom. Then, using a clean ruler or side of a large knife, gently press and flatten each side of the log—slightly angled and pointing upward—to complete the triangle (similar to the shape of a Toblerone chocolate bar). Wrap the dough loosely in wax paper, and chill in the refrigerator for 30 minutes. Remove and cut the triangle log of dough into ½-inch-thick triangles. Arrange them on buttered baking sheets about 1 inch apart, and top each piece with a hazelnut half. Bake on the middle shelf of the oven in batches for 18 to 20 minutes, or until golden. Cool on racks, and store in airtight containers. Yield: 24 cookies.

King's cookies (KONINGSKOEKJES)

These cookies with their gold, glistening topping of citron look like king's jewels. They are crunchy and chewy and just delicious.

1¾ cups all-purpose flour
11 tablespoons unsalted butter, cold, cut into pats
¼ teaspoon finely textured salt
1 cup loosely packed light brown sugar
2 teaspoons lemon zest
1 egg, lightly beaten
½ cup sliced almonds
½ cup candied citron, finely chopped (available on amazon.com or at holiday time in local supermarkets)

Preheat oven to 350°F. In a food processor fitted with a metal blade, mix flour, butter, salt, sugar, and zest, until a cohesive dough forms. Transfer to a lightly floured work surface, knead a few times to get the dough soft and pliable, then roll or pat into a 9-inch square. Neatly brush on half of the beaten egg, and evenly sprinkle with the sliced almonds and citron. With your rolling pin, roll the toppings very lightly into the dough. Brush with the remaining egg. Cut into 6 (1½-inch) strips and then into 30 (1½-inch-square) cookies. Place on lightly greased baking sheets, and bake in batches for about 20 minutes, or until golden. Turn oven off and allow cookies to stand for 5 minutes more. Cool on racks, and store in airtight containers. Yield: 30 cookies.

Meringue sticks dipped in chocolate (BOKKEPOOTJES)

Every year, in early January, our dear friend and cooking teacher/food writer/food historian Stephen Schmidt joins us for a weekend in the country. All we do during that time is talk about food and cook and eat. Last year, Steve helped me make these Dutch meringue cookies and actually wrote the recipe. The Dutch name *bokkepootjes* means goat legs. Note: You'll need a pastry bag and a plain round tip.

COOKIE STICKS:

1 cup (about 4 ounces) plus ¼ cup sliced almonds, divided

½ cup plus ⅓ cup granulated sugar, divided

2 tablespoons all-purpose flour

3 egg whites (from large eggs), room temperature

FILLING:

1 cup confectioners' sugar

2 tablespoons unsalted butter, softened

¼ teaspoon finely textured salt

¼ teaspoon grated lemon zest

Lemon juice, as needed

COATING:

6 ounces semisweet chocolate

Preheat oven to 325°F. Place shelves in the lower and upper part of the oven. Line two baking sheets with parchment paper, and if necessary, cut the paper to cover the sheet bottoms with overlapping the sides. Set aside.

PREPARE THE COOKIE STICKS: In a food processor, grind almonds, ½ cup sugar, and flour to a fine powder. Set aside. In an electric mixer, beat egg whites at medium speed until they form soft peaks. Add about 1 teaspoon of the remaining ⅓ cup sugar, and beat whites until stiff. Gradually sprinkle in the remainder of the ⅓ cup sugar, and beat until the whites are very stiff and glossy, about 2 minutes. Sprinkle ground almond mixture over egg whites and gently fold together using a rubber spatula in an under-over motion. Don't overwork the mixture. Spoon batter into a pastry bag fitted with a ½-inch plain round tip. On the prepared sheets, pipe sticks 2½ inches long, about 1 inch apart. Using your fingers, break the remaining ¼ cup of almonds into rough ¼-inch pieces. Sprinkle the bits on the sticks.

BAKE THE STICKS: Place baking sheets in the oven and bake for 15 minutes. Move the baking sheet on the top shelf to the bottom shelf, and vice versa. Also rotate each sheet front to back. Continue baking, about 5 to 10 minutes longer, until the sticks are golden brown and come away easily from the paper liners without sticking. Let the sticks cool on the sheets for 2 minutes.Then with a metal spatula scrape them off the parchment and transfer them to racks to cool completely. If you have not used all of the batter and need to bake more sticks, wipe the parchment paper clean with a paper towel before piping more, and repeating the baking process.

Meringue sticks dipped in chocolate ***(Bokkepootjes)***

MAKE THE FILLING: In a small bowl, mash confectioners' sugar, butter, salt, and zest with the back of a wooden spoon until the mixture becomes a stiff, crumbly paste. Work in just enough lemon juice by drops to make the dough smooth and spreadable but still very stiff, like the filling of a store-bought sandwich cookie. Spread the flat side of one of the cooled cookie sticks with a ⅛-inch thick layer of filling. Place another cookie stick flat side down on top of the filling and gently press to make the two cookies stick together.

MAKE THE COATING: Melt chocolate in a shallow bowl in the microwave. Start with 30 seconds, remove, and stir; repeat for 20 seconds, then 10 seconds at a time, until completely melted. Carefully remove bowl from the microwave. Dip ¾ inch of each end of each cookie into the melted chocolate and remove with a twist. Place each coated stick on parchment-lined baking sheets. Refrigerate until the chocolate hardens. Store in airtight containers at room temperature. Yield: 18 to 20 cookies

Orange diamonds ('WENER PUNTJES)

The diamond-shaped cookies made with orange zest and an orange glaze look very nice on a cookie tray, but if you prefer to make them more Christmas-y, you can, of course, color them red or green.

11 tablespoons unsalted butter, softened
¼ teaspoon finely textured salt
2 egg yolks
½ cup packed light brown sugar
½ cup granulated sugar
1¾ cups all-purpose flour
1 orange, zested
1⅓ cup confectioners' sugar
2 to 3 tablespoons freshly squeezed orange juice, strained
Red and yellow food coloring, if desired

Preheat oven to 350°F. In an electric mixer, cream butter, salt, and yolks, then add both sugars, combining well. Mix in flour and zest until a cohesive dough forms. Spread the dough on a buttered baking sheet, and using a spatula make a neat rectangle and carefully roll out with a floured rolling pin to a 9x11-inch rectangle. Bake for 25 minutes, or until light golden. In a small bowl, mix confectioner's sugar with orange juice, 1 tablespoon at a time. If desired, add food coloring to create a nice shade of orange. Remove baking sheet from the oven. While still warm, spread the glaze, and with a sharp knife cut into neat diamond-shaped cookies. Cook on racks, and store in airtight containers. Yield: 30 to 36 diamonds.

Sugared puff pastry ovals

In Dutch, these cookies are called *Arnhemse meisjes* or girls from the city of Arnhem. In the late nineteenth century, an ambitious Dutch-American baker in Albany, New York, called his version *Albimaids*.

2 sheets frozen puff pastry, thawed (I use Pepperidge Farm brand)
2 cups granulated sugar

Preheat oven to 375°F. On a lightly floured work surface, using a rolling pin, roll the sheets to make 10x 9½-inch rectangles and with a 2½-inch round cutter cut 10 rounds out of each sheet. On a piece of wax paper spread 1 cup of sugar in a thick layer. Working quickly in small batches, place the dough rounds on the sugar, sprinkle them generously with sugar, and use a rolling pin to roll them out into 4-inch flat oval shapes. As soon as they are rolled out, prick the ovals all over with a fork, arrange them on lightly buttered baking sheets about 1 inch apart, and bake in batches on the middle shelf of the oven for 12 to 15 minutes, or until they are lightly golden. Cool on racks, and store in airtight containers. Note: For best results do not combine and re-roll scraps. Instead, cut scraps into small, even strips; brush with egg wash and sprinkle with salt and pepper. Bake, as indicated above, to make small salty bites as accompaniments to a glass of wine or beer. Yield: 20 cookies.

Tea cookjes (THEE KOEKJES)

Please note the half English-half Dutch spelling of the word *cookjes* in the title of this recipe. The recipe comes from the hand-written cookbook of Maria Sanders van Rensselaer (1749–1830), wife of Philip van Rensselaer of Cherry Hill in Albany, New York. The Van Rensselaer house is now a historic museum. Even though the cookies are made from such simple ingredients, "you cannot eat just one." They are positively addictive. Making these buttery, hard, crisp cookies is a great parent-child project, and little gift bags tied with red ribbons, are a festive addition to each place setting at your holiday table.

16 tablespoons (2 sticks) unsalted butter, softened
½ teaspoon finely textured salt
1½ cups granulated sugar
¾ cup cold water
3½ cups all-purpose flour

Preheat oven to 350°F. In an electric mixer, cream butter and salt while adding sugar a little at a time. Continue creaming and add water alternately with flour. Cover dough in plastic wrap, and refrigerate for 1 hour. Roll dough into ½-inch balls. Arrange them on buttered baking sheets about ½ inch apart, and bake in batches for 16 to 18 minutes, or until lightly browned at the edges and on the bottom. Cool on racks, and store in airtight containers. Yield: at least 10 dozen cookies.

Oliebollen
Recipe on page 78

Recipes for the New Year's Celebration

Deep-fried apple slices *(Appelflappen)*

Deep-fried filled dough I *(Oliekoecken)*

Deep-fried filled dough II *(Oliebollen)*

Deep-fried snowballs with chocolate sauce (S*neeuwballen met chocolade saus)*

Mixed cooked vegetable salad *(Huzarensla)*

New Year's cakes *(NieuwJaarskoeken)*

One-pot meal of french-cut pole or green beans, marrow beans, potatoes, bacon, and sausage (*Naakte kindertjes in het gras)*

Pickled herring salad *(Haringsla)*

Ask any Dutch person "what do you like to eat on New Year's Eve?" and the answer is guaranteed to be "*oliebollen* or *appelflappen*." These deep-fried treats have been a part of the celebration on the last day of the year for a long time. Dutch Master Albert Cuyp (1620–1691) painted a lovely depiction, now in the Dordrecht Museum, of a woman with a red ware bowl of *olie-koecken*. We can think of it as proof they were already made in the 1600s. Further proof is a recipe for a rich version that contains whole almonds in the 1683 edition of *The Sensible Cook*. The first four recipes in this chapter are for these deep-fried treats, together with some other traditional specialties, to celebrate the last day of the old and the beginning of the new year.

Deep-fried apple slices (APPELFLAPPEN)

We'll begin the array with apple slices, dipped in cinnamon-sugar, batter, and deep fried—a delicious version of an apple beignet. My sister-in-law was known for these; visitors to her house on New Year's Day knew these would be waiting.

½ cup warm (100°F to 110°F) water
1 package active dry yeast
½ teaspoon plus 6 tablespoons granulated sugar, divided use
4 to 5 medium Golden Delicious apples
1½ cups all-purpose flour
Pinch finely textured salt
1¼ cups whole milk
2 teaspoons ground cinnamon
Oil, for deep frying
Confectioners' sugar

Pour warm water into a small bowl and sprinkle with yeast and ½ teaspoon sugar. Let stand for a moment, then stir to dissolve yeast. Set aside in a warm place. Peel, core, and cut apples crosswise into ½-inch thick slices. In a large bowl, combine flour, salt, and half the milk. When yeast has risen and is bubbly, add it to flour mixture and stir to make a smooth batter. Stir in the remaining milk. Cover bowl and allow to rise for

1 hour. Once batter has risen, heat oil to 350°F. Combine cinnamon and remaining sugar on a plate and dip 3 or 4 apple slices at a time into the mixture to lightly coat each side, shaking off any excess. Then dip slices into the batter, coating both sides. Use tongs to carefully slide each slice into the hot oil. Fry them until golden brown on both sides. Gently remove the puffed apple slices with tongs or a long metal skewer, trying not to puncture the coating. Drain in a colander, then on paper towels. Repeat with remaining apple slices. While still warm, dust with confectioners' sugar. Serve immediately. Yield: 24 to 28 apple beignets.

Deep-fried filled dough I (OLIEKOECKEN)

This is an outstanding version of a deep-fried pastry that came from the 1683 edition of *De Verstandige Kok (The Sensible Cook)*. I added my own touch by adding a little sugar to the mix. Note: When making a large number of *oliekoecken* for a party, it is better to cut them in halves or quarters for serving, rather than make them in a smaller size. The almonds and apple pieces tend to distribute unevenly in miniature ones.

½ cup warm (100°F to 110°F) water
3 packages active dry yeast
Pinch plus ⅓ cup granulated sugar
8 tablespoons (1 stick) unsalted butter
1¾ cups raisins
4 cups all-purpose flour
1 tablespoon ground cinnamon
½ teaspoon ground cloves
½ teaspoon ground ginger
¼ teaspoon finely textured salt
1½ cups whole milk
1 cup whole unblanched almonds
3 medium Granny Smith apples, peeled, cored and cut into small slivers
Oil, for frying
Confectioners' or granulated sugar, optional

Pour warm water into a small bowl and sprinkle with yeast and sugar. Let stand for a minute, then stir to dissolve yeast. Set aside in a warm place. Melt butter on the stove or in the microwave, and let cool. Place raisins in a saucepan, cover with water, and boil for 1 minute. Remove from heat, cool for 5 minutes, then drain. Pat dry with paper towels and mix with 1 tablespoon of flour. Place remaining flour in a large bowl, stir in cinnamon, cloves, ginger, and salt. Make a well in the middle and pour in yeast mixture. Stirring from the middle, slowly add melted butter and milk. Continue to stir until flour is completely incorporated and a very stiff batter forms. Thoroughly mix in raisins, almonds, and apples. Cover bowl and allow batter to rise for about 1 hour, or until doubled, then stir down. Heat about 4 inches oil to 350°F in a large pot, or use a deep fryer. My mother taught me that *olie-koecken* should "swim in the oil." Using an ice cream scoop or large spoon, scoop a 2-inch wide spoonful of batter. Holding the scoop or spoon just above the oil, carefully push the batter off with another spoon to make as round a ball as possible. Fry in batches of 4 or 5 at a time for about 5 minutes on each side, or until golden brown. Check for doneness by cutting into one. Drain on paper towels. The original recipe does not call for sprinkling or rolling them in sugar. But while they are very good plain, you can certainly dust them with confectioners' sugar or roll them in granulated sugar. Yield: about 36.

Deep-fried filled dough II (OLIEBOLLEN)

Here is my Mother's version of *olie-koecken*, nowadays called *oliebollen*. Hers are filled with apple, raisins, currants, and candied mixed fruit, which is currently more customary.

½ cup warm (100°F to 110 °F) water
3 packages active dry yeast
Pinch granulated sugar
½ cup raisins
½ cup currants (see note, page 46)
4 cups all-purpose flour
¼ teaspoon finely textured salt
1½ cups whole milk
1 cup candied mixed fruits
3 medium Granny Smith apples, peeled, cored and cut into small slivers
Oil, for deep frying
Confectioners' sugar

Pour warm water into a small bowl and sprinkle with yeast and sugar. Let stand for a minute, then stir to dissolve yeast. Set aside in a warm place. Place raisins and currants in a saucepan, cover with water, and boil for 1 minute. Remove from heat, cool for 5 minutes, then drain. Pat dry with paper towels and mix with 1 tablespoon of flour. Place remaining flour in a large bowl, stir in salt. Make a well in the middle and pour in yeast mixture. Stirring from the middle, slowly add milk, and continue to stir until flour is completely incorporated and a very stiff batter forms. Thoroughly mix in raisins, currants, candied mixed fruit, and apples. Cover bowl and allow the batter to rise for about

Deep-fried filled dough II *(Oliebollen)*

1 hour, or until doubled, then stir down. Heat about 4 inches oil to 350°F in a large pot, or use a deep fryer. My mother said that *oliebollen*, like *oliekoecken*, should "swim in the oil" too. Using an ice cream scoop or large spoon, scoop a 2-inch wide spoonful of batter. Holding the scoop or spoon just above the oil, carefully push the batter off with another spoon to make as round a ball as possible. Fry in batches of 4 or 5 at a time for about 5 minutes on each side, or until golden brown. Check for doneness by cutting into one. Drain on paper towels. Roll in confectioners' sugar. Yield: about 36.

Deep-fried snowballs with chocolate sauce

(SNEEUWBALLEN MET CHOCOLADE SAUS)

My mother, a soft-hearted woman and an excellent cook, would generally make both oliebollen and appelflappen, but when I would beg her, she would also make these *sneeuwballen* for New Year's Day.

FOR THE SNOWBALLS:

1 cup water

4 tablespoons unsalted butter

⅛ teaspoon finely textured salt

½ cup all-purpose flour

2 eggs

Oil, for deep frying

Confectioners' sugar

FOR THE CHOCOLATE SAUCE:

2 cups whole milk

2 tablespoons cornstarch

¼ cup cocoa powder (I use Droste brand; available on amazon.com)

Scant ¼ cup granulated sugar

MAKE THE SNOWBALLS: In a saucepan, combine water, butter, and salt and bring to a boil. When the butter has melted, sift the flour over the mixture and turn the heat down to low. Stir until a cohesive dough forms and a light film forms on the bottom of the pan. Remove from heat, cool for 5 minutes, then add one egg at a time, stirring until completely incorporated. Stir for 5 minutes until the dough is light and airy. Heat oil to 350°F. Use two spoons to form 1½-inch balls, and carefully drop into the hot oil. The balls will "magically" expand or puff. Fry until golden brown. Use a slotted spoon to remove, and drain in a colander, then on paper towels.

MAKE THE CHOCOLATE SAUCE: In a small saucepan, bring 1¾ cups of milk to a boil. In a small bowl, mix cornstarch, cocoa, and sugar, stir in remaining milk until the sauce is smooth. When the milk boils, turn down the heat and add the chocolate sauce. Continue stirring for 2 minutes. Remove and pour into bowl or pitcher. Cover lightly with plastic wrap to prevent a film from forming. This is sauce is great on ice cream, too.

TO SERVE: Sift confectioners' sugar over the snowballs, and serve warm or cold. If you really want to gild the lily, fill each snowball—either by cutting open or using a piping bag—with sweetened whipped cream. Serve with the chocolate sauce on the side. Yield: 18 snowballs.

Mixed cooked vegetable salad (HUZARENSLA)

In the Netherlands, a late-night supper is often served on New Year's Eve. When I grew up, my parents would open a bottle of champagne at the stroke of midnight and have a delicious little "souper." It often featured an entrée salad that could easily be made ahead—such as this vegetable salad, or both the vegetable and herring salads (see recipe, page 85). Serve with whole grain rolls and butter, and of course plenty of the bubbly. In our house, my father would make the *huzarensla* for the occasion. It always was round, flattened, and looked like the face of a clock with the hands set for almost midnight. Make the salad the day before serving, so the flavors have a chance to marry, and decorate it on serving day.

FOR THE SALAD:

4 cups boiled Maine or Yukon potatoes, peeled and diced

4 cups cooked mixed vegetables, such as peas, carrots, and green beans, diced, if necessary

Huzarensla, ready for a midnight supper on New Year's Eve.

3 medium Golden Delicious apples, peeled, cored and diced
1 large cucumber, peeled, seeded, cut diced
2 cups cooked beef, cubed (leftover roast is good), optional
¾ cup mayonnaise (use a good commercial brand)
2 hard-boiled eggs, mashed
2 tablespoons white distilled vinegar
Salt and freshly ground black pepper, to taste

FOR DECORATION:
Mayonnaise (use a good commercial brand), as needed
Boston lettuce leaves

FOR A CLOCK FACE:
6 black pitted olives or cherry tomatoes, cut in half
2 strips red pepper or 2 green beans
Sweet and sour gherkins
Hard-boiled eggs, peeled and sliced
Cherry tomatoes

MAKE THE SALAD: In a large bowl, combine potatoes, vegetables, apples, cucumber and beef, if desired. In a small bowl, thoroughly combine mayonnaise, eggs, vinegar, salt, and pepper, then lightly dress the mixed vegetables. A little more mayonnaise may be needed to hold the salad nicely together. Taste and adjust seasonings, if necessary. Refrigerate overnight. Taste, and add more vinegar, if needed.

TO SERVE: Mound salad on a platter, then flatten it. Spread with mayonnaise. Place Boston lettuce leaves around the base of the salad. To make the clock face: Place the olive or cherry tomato halves on the salad to indicate the numbers of the clock and add the pepper strips or green beans as hands of the clock set at almost 12 o'clock.

DECORATE: Take sweet-and-sour gherkins, cut them in a fan shape by slicing them in three parts from the top but not all the way through, and fan them out adding egg slices and cherry tomatoes. For a more elaborate presentation, surround the salad with some of the Dutch hors' d'oeuvres from chapter 8. Yield: Serves at least 8, depending on accompaniments.

New Year's cakes (NIEUWJAARSKOEKEN)

In the seventeenth-century Dutch colony in North America, New Netherland, New Year's cakes were traditionally served in large quantities on New Year's Day, which was a day for visiting. There are many nineteenth-century references to this tradition. I found the original in a hand-written cookbook of Maria Lotts Lefferts (1786–1865) of Brooklyn, New York. I have tinkered with this recipe for years. I have finally come to the conclusion that rolling the dough into 1-inch balls and flattening the balls with the floured bottom of a glass is the easiest, but if you prefer roll them with a rolling pin, make the sheet as thin as possible and cut with a 2-inch round cutter. You'll love the combination of caraway and orange zest as the flavoring.

2 cups all-purpose flour

½ cup packed light brown sugar

¼ teaspoon baking soda

½ teaspoon finely textured salt

8 tablespoons (1 stick) unsalted butter

1 egg, lightly beaten

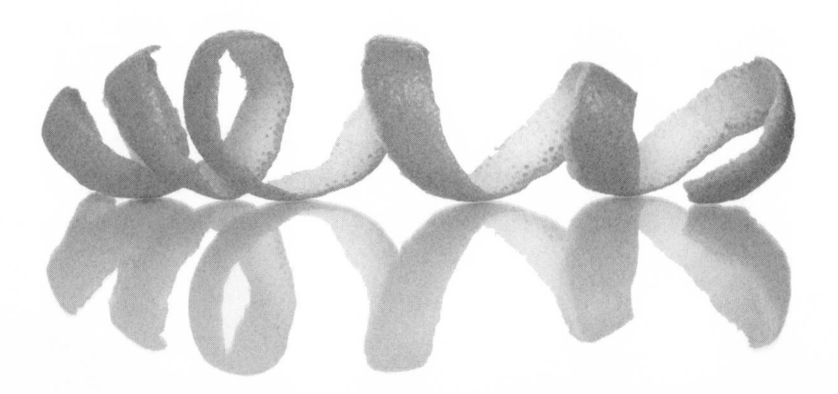

¼ cup whole milk

1½ teaspoons caraway seed, crushed somewhat with a rolling pin to release flavor

1½ tablespoons orange zest

Preheat oven to 300°F. Sift all dry ingredients into a large bowl. A neat trick, if the sugar is too lumpy, is to rub it between your hands first, then push it through the sifter. In a food processor fitted with a metal blade, pulse dry ingredients and butter until the mixture looks like coarse meal. In a small bowl or measuring cup, beat the egg and milk. Add it to the food processor along with seeds and zest. Process until the dough becomes cohesive. Cover in plastic wrap, and cool in the refrigerator for 1 hour. On a floured work surface, roll dough into 1-inch balls. Then flatten as thin as possible with the bottom of a floured glass. Carefully transfer to buttered baking sheets, and bake in batches for about 25 to 30 minutes, or until pale brown and crisp. Yield: at least 4 dozen, depending on size.

Typical Dutch one-pot meal

One-pot meal of french-cut pole or green beans, marrow beans, potatoes, bacon, and sausage (NAAKTE KINDERTJES IN HET GRAS)

The name of this recipe in Dutch means "naked children in the grass"—the marrow beans are the children and the pole beans the grass. In many Dutch families, particularly in the northern province of Groningen, this one-pot meal is eaten on New Year's Day to offset the aftereffects of too many toasts to the new year. It is a very old recipe, and was originally made with green beans that had been salt preserved for the winter. You can omit the sausage, if desired. But if used, cook the sausage together with the potatoes and green beans to ensure none of the flavorful juices are lost.

½ pound marrow beans (small dried white beans) or substitute small white canned beans

½ medium yellow onion, peeled

2 pounds Maine or Yukon potatoes, peeled and diced

1 pound pole beans, french cut (or substitute 2 packages frozen french cut green beans, thawed)

1 pound smoked sausage, if desired

1 pound bacon, diced

4 tablespoons butter

4 ounces light cream or whole milk

Salt and freshly ground black pepper

Rinse the marrow beans and pick them over to remove any small stones or other foreign matter. Place the beans in a large saucepan, and cover with water to about 1-inch above the beans. Bring to a boil. Turn off the heat, and let them soak for 1 hour. Add the onion and simmer for 2 to 3 hours. Marrow beans tend to need a lot of time, but do not overcook—they should be tender, but not mushy. Drain and set aside. Or if using canned beans, drain, and set aside (but do not use the onion if using canned beans). In a large pot, boil the potatoes and pole or green beans together until tender, placing the sausage, if used, on top. Drain and save the cooking water. Set the beans, potatoes, and sausage aside, but keep them warm. In the same pot, lightly brown the bacon pieces. Drain off most of the fat and discard or save for another purpose. Add the butter to the bacon and melt. Add the potatoes and pole beans, cream, and salt and pepper, to taste. Mash with a potato masher until creamy, then stir in the marrow or canned beans. Taste, and re-season, if necessary. If the mixture is too thick, thin it with some of the reserved water. Slice the sausage, place on top, and serve. Yield: 4 to 6 large servings.

Pickled herring salad (HARINGSLA)

Herring, once the "pillar of Dutch wealth," is used pickled in this salad that often is served as a late-night supper on New Year's Eve, but tastes good anytime.

FOR THE SALAD:

1½ pounds pickled herring, drained and diced small

2 Granny Smith apples, peeled, cored, and diced small

¾ pound boiled beets, drained, and diced small

1½ pounds (4 to 6) Maine or Yukon potatoes, peeled, boiled, and diced small

1 cucumber, peeled, seeded, and diced small

1 medium yellow onion, peeled and chopped

2 eggs, hard-boiled and peeled

Salt and freshly ground black pepper, to taste

½ cup mayonnaise, or more as needed (use a good commercial brand)

FOR THE GARNISH:

6 to 8 Boston lettuce leaves

2 eggs, hard-boiled and peeled, whites and yolks mashed separately

1 bunch fresh parsley

2 eggs, hard-boiled, peeled and cut in eighths

Pickled pearl onions (the kind used in martinis)

In a large bowl, combine the herring, apples, beets, potatoes, cucumber, and onion. In a small bowl, mash eggs, add salt and pepper, to taste, and stir in mayonnaise. Add the mashed eggs to the herring and vegetables. Combine thoroughly. You may need to add more mayonnaise at this point to bind the mixture nicely, but do not overdo. Refrigerate. When ready to serve, mound the herring salad on a platter and surround it with the lettuce leaves. Cover one side of the mound with mashed egg white and the other side with mashed egg yolks, and where they meet in the middle, place small parsley bouquets. Surround the salad with egg wedges, and place the pearl onions around the base. Yield: 6 to 8 servings.

Puff pastry sticks with curry and peanuts

Recipes for Savory Cookies

Caraway bows *(Karwijzaad strikjes)*

Cheese cookies *(Kaaskoekjes)*

Dilly cheese buttons *(Zoute knopen met dille)*

Hazelnut cheese cookies *(Hazelnoot-en kaaskoekjes)*

Puff pastry sticks with

- Cheese and sesame seeds *(Kaasstengels met sesamzaad)*
- Curry and peanuts *(Kerrie en pindastengels)*
- Whole almonds *(Amandelstengels)*

Salmon buttons *(Zoute knopen met gerookte zalm)*

Salty balls *(Zoute bollen)*

Savory or salty cookies, *zoutjes* ("salties") have a long tradition in Holland. You're seldom offered a drink without something to nibble with it, whether it is a baked good or just salty nuts or chips. Dutch bakery and grocery shops generally have a nice variety of salty cookies, and here are some examples for you to try at home.

Caraway bows (KARWIJZAAD STRIKJES)

This recipe makes an attractive accompaniment to a glass of wine or beer.

2 cups all-purpose flour

1 teaspoon baking powder

1 teaspoon finely textured salt

5 tablespoons unsalted butter

5 tablespoons (3 ounces) cream cheese

1 egg plus 1 egg white

Caraway seed, as desired

Sea salt, to taste

In a food processor fitted with a metal blade, pulse flour, baking powder, salt, butter, cream cheese, and egg, until a smooth dough forms. Cover in plastic wrap, and refrigerate. After 30 minutes, preheat oven to 400 °F. Place dough between 2 sheets of wax paper, and roll into a 12x6-inch rectangle. Cut in half lengthwise, then into 1x3-inch pieces. Brush with egg white and sprinkle heavily with caraway and lightly with sea salt. Press and twist each piece in the middle so it looks like a bow tie. Arrange them on lightly buttered baking sheets, and bake in batches for about 15 minutes, or until golden. Yield: 24 bows.

Cheese cookies *(Kaaskoekjes)*

Cheese cookies (KAASKOEKJES)

Savory cheese cookies and some crunchy salted nuts are the perfect accompaniments to a glass of red wine and will perk rather than deaden the appetite for the dinner to come. The recipe that follows is a very simple but tasty example of cheese cookies.

1 cup all-purpose flour

¼ teaspoon finely textured salt

7 tablespoons unsalted butter

1 cup grated Gouda cheese

Salt and freshly ground white pepper

Preheat oven to 350°F. In a food processor, pulse all ingredients until a cohesive dough forms. Roll into a 10-inch log, then cut into 40 (¼-inch) rounds. Place on buttered baking sheets, and bake in batches for about 20 minutes, until light golden. Do not overbake or they will become bitter. Yield: 40 cookies.

Dilly cheese buttons (ZOUTE KNOPEN MET DILLE)

These buttons make a quick, easy, and delicious tray-passed hors d'oeuvre. Use this recipe to make your own dilly cheese filling, or purchase a pre-made filling, such as Boursin brand cheese.

FOR THE DOUGH:

1 cup all-purpose flour

1 teaspoon baking powder

6 tablespoons butter

1 cup grated Gouda cheese

¼ teaspoon finely textured salt

3 tablespoons finely chopped dill

¼ teaspoon freshly ground black pepper

FOR THE FILLING:

4 ounces cream cheese

½ cup combined finely chopped dill, parsley, and scallions

2 to 3 tablespoons cream or whole milk

Salt and freshly ground black pepper, to taste

MAKE THE DOUGH: Preheat oven to 350°F. In a food processor fitted with a metal blade, combine all ingredients until a cohesive dough forms. Roll into 1-inch balls. Place on buttered baking sheets. With your forefinger, make an indent in each ball to create a well. Then with the palm of your hand, neatly press dough down to slightly flatten repairing any cracks, if needed. Bake in batches for 25 minutes, or until light golden brown. Cool on racks.

MAKE THE DILLY CHEESE FILLING: In an electric mixer, beat cream cheese until fluffy, then add the herbs. If necessary, thin with cream or milk. Stir in salt and pepper, to taste. Transfer to an airtight container and refrigerate. This cheese mixture is also great with crackers.

TO SERVE: Fill the small well in each button with 1 teaspoon or so of the dilly cheese filling or store-bought Boursin cheese. Yield: 15 to 18 buttons.

Hazelnut cheese cookies (HAZELNOOT-EN KAASKOEKJES)

This is your introduction to Old Amsterdam cheese, an aged Gouda-style cheese with a black, not a red, wax coating. This cheese is so delicious, look for it in cheese shops or ask your grocer. It has a sweet and nutty flavor and is particularly good paired with the hazelnuts in these cookies. It is also wonderful in a cheese sauce, giving macaroni and cheese a whole new dimension.

1¼ cups all-purpose flour

8 tablespoons (1 stick) unsalted butter

1 egg yolk

1 cup grated Old Amsterdam, or other aged cheese

2 tablespoons water

½ teaspoon finely textured salt

¼ teaspoon freshly ground black pepper

¼ cup finely chopped hazelnuts

Preheat oven to 350°F. In a food processor fitted with a metal blade, combine all ingredients except for nuts, until a cohesive dough forms. Add hazelnuts and pulse to combine. Lightly flour a work surface, and knead dough until all ingredients are evenly distributed. With a floured rolling pin, roll dough into a ⅛-inch thick sheet, or thinner if possible. Using a 2-inch round cutter, cut out cookies. Place on baking sheets, and bake in batches for 20 minutes, until light golden on the bottom. Cool on racks, and store in airtight containers. To refresh the cookies reheat for 8 to 10 minutes in a 300°F oven. Yield: at least 24 cookies

Puff pastry sticks with cheese and sesame seeds

(KAASSTENGELS MET SESAMZAAD)

This recipe and the two that follow, use frozen puff pastry to speed up preparation time. After you make this recipe once, you will think up your own toppings! These sticks can be served with drinks, but are also very nice with a cup of soup as part of a first course.

1 sheet frozen puff pastry, thawed (I use Pepperidge Farm brand)

1 egg, beaten with a fork

½ cup to 1 cup grated pepper jack cheese

½ cup sesame seeds

Preheat oven to 400°F. On a lightly floured work surface, unfold the thawed sheet and you will see three folds; leave intact and place the sheet with the wide side toward you on the counter, then cut into three parts along the folds. Carefully brush with the beaten egg and heavily sprinkle with the grated cheese and sesame seeds. Use a flat, clean plastic ruler, start on top, press down and cut across into sticks of ¾-inch wide. (The ruler helps the topping to adhere). Transfer to buttered baking sheets and bake in batches for 12 to 15 minutes, or until puffed and golden. Cool and store in an airtight box. Yield: 36 to 42 sticks.

Puff pastry sticks with curry and peanuts (KERRIE EN PINDASTENGELS)

1 sheet frozen puff pastry, thawed

1 egg, beaten with a fork

Sea salt

Medium spiced curry powder

½ to 1 cup finely chopped peanuts

Preheat oven to 400°F. On a lightly floured work surface, unfold the sheet and you will see three folds; leave intact and place the sheet with the wide side toward you on the counter, then cut into three parts along the folds. Carefully brush with beaten egg, sprinkle with salt, heavily sprinkle with curry powder, then cover with peanuts. Using a flat, clean plastic ruler, start on top, press down and cut across into sticks of ¾-inch wide. (The ruler helps the topping to adhere). Place on buttered baking sheets and bake in batches for 12 to 15 minutes, or until puffed and golden. Cool on racks, and store in airtight containers. Yield: 36 to 42 sticks.

Puff pastry sticks with whole almonds (AMANDELSTENGELS)

1½ cups whole blanched almonds

1 sheet frozen puff pastry, thawed

1 egg, beaten with a fork

Sea salt

Preheat oven to 300°F. Place the almonds on a baking sheet, and bake for 15 minutes. Remove, and set aside. Increase heat to 400°F. On a lightly floured work surface unfold the sheet and you will see three folds; leave intact and place the sheet with the wide side

toward you on the counter, then cut into three parts along the folds. Carefully brush with the beaten egg and lightly sprinkle with the sea salt. Carefully place nine almonds neatly end-to-end across, in rows all the way down the pastry sheets. Use a flat, clean plastic ruler, start on top, press down and cut across into sticks of ¾-inch wide and 3⅓-inch long. (The ruler helps the topping to adhere). Brush carefully with beaten egg. Place sticks on buttered baking sheets, and bake in batches for 12 to 15 minutes or until puffed and golden. Cool on racks, and store in airtight containers. Yield per sheet: 36 to 42 sticks.

Salmon buttons (ZOUTE KNOPEN MET GEROOKTE ZALM)

Similar in shape to the dilly cheese buttons, these buttons make an impressive hors d'oeuvre, or, together with a small salad, could be served as a starter to a festive meal. The filling is also great with crackers.

FOR THE BUTTONS:

1 cup all-purpose flour

1 teaspoon baking powder

6 tablespoons unsalted butter

3 ounces smoked salmon, divided in half to be used for both the dough and the filling, finely chopped

¼ teaspoon finely textured salt

¼ teaspoon freshly ground black pepper

SALMON CHEESE FILLING:

4 ounces cream cheese

Remaining finely chopped salmon

2 to 3 tablespoons cream or milk

Salt and freshly ground black pepper, to taste

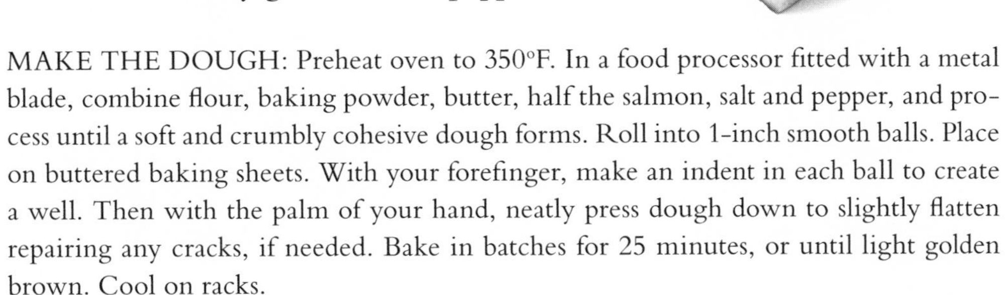

MAKE THE DOUGH: Preheat oven to 350°F. In a food processor fitted with a metal blade, combine flour, baking powder, butter, half the salmon, salt and pepper, and process until a soft and crumbly cohesive dough forms. Roll into 1-inch smooth balls. Place on buttered baking sheets. With your forefinger, make an indent in each ball to create a well. Then with the palm of your hand, neatly press dough down to slightly flatten repairing any cracks, if needed. Bake in batches for 25 minutes, or until light golden brown. Cool on racks.

MAKE THE FILLING: In an electric mixer, beat cream cheese until fluffy, add salmon, and thin as necessary with cream or milk. Taste before adding salt and pepper, as commercially smoked salmon is quite salty. Transfer to an airtight container and refrigerate.

TO SERVE: Fill the small well in each button with 1 teaspoon or so of the salmon cheese filling. Yield: 18 to 20 buttons.

Salty balls (ZOUTE BOLLEN)

These small, simple cookies are the most typical example of Dutch savory cookies. Try to make perfectly round balls.

2 cups plus 1 tablespoon all-purpose flour

10 tablespoons unsalted butter

1¾ teaspoons finely textured salt

1 egg, lightly beaten with a fork

Preheat oven to 350°F. In a food processor outfitted with a metal blade, combine flour, butter, salt and egg and process until a cohesive dough forms. Roll into perfectly smooth balls (press together any cracks), a little bigger than a marble and place on buttered baking sheets. Bake in batches for 30 to 35 minutes, until light brown. Cool on racks, and store in airtight containers. Yield: 40 balls.

Traditional Dutch snack platter *(Bittergarnituur)*
Recipe on page 97

Recipes for Savory Party Treats

Dutch cheese board *(Hollandse kaasplank)*

Traditional Dutch snack platter (*Bittergarnituur)*

Calf's ears *(Kalfsoren)*

Cheese balls *(Kaasballetjes)*

Cheese puffs (*Kaassoesjes)*

Croquette balls and croquettes *(Bitterballen en kroketten)*

Deviled eggs *(Gevulde eieren)*

Flavored savory butters:

- Cheese butter *(Kaasboter)*
- Herb butter *(Kruidenboter)*
- Shrimp butter *(Garnalenboter)*

Ham and asparagus rolls *(Ham en asperge rolletjes)*

Ham puffs (*Hamsoesjes)*

Sausage rolls *(Saucijzenbroodjes)*

Shrimp salad in plum tomatoes *(Gevulde tomaatjes met garnalensla)*

Smoked mackerel paté *(Gerookte makreel paté)*

Let's begin this chapter of savory treats, snacks, and hors d'oeuvres with a discussion of a Dutch cheese board and the quintessential Dutch snack platter. More delicious old and new recipes will follow.

Dutch cheese platter ***(Hollandse kaasplank)***

Dutch cheese platter (HOLLANDSE KAASPLANK)

To make a Dutch cheese platter you obviously need Dutch cheeses. The Netherlands has a large variety of cheeses, but many are not available in America. Therefore, I suggest this selection, each of which can be purchased here. Choose at least 2 or 3 for your cheese board:

GOUDA: a smooth, rich cheese which has a red wax coating and is available in mild, medium and aged versions, and can be served cubed or sliced.

OLD AMSTERDAM OR BEEMSTER: has a black wax coating and is an aged Gouda-style cheese with a slightly sweet, nutty flavor; for a cheese board it is best sliced rather than cubed.

GOAT GOUDA *(Geitenkaas)*: is a hard rather than creamy goat cheese and can be served cubed or sliced.

EDAM: shaped in the familiar ball with red wax coating is a mild cheese made from skimmed milk, and can be served cubed or sliced.

CLOVE CHEESE (*Nagelkaas)*: as the name indicates contains whole cloves to make a very flavorful medium-aged cheese, best served cubed.

LEYDEN CUMIN CHEESE *(Komijne kaas)*: is heavily spiced with cumin seed and is best for a cheese board sliced rather than cubed.

You might add your favorite blue cheese or an herb cheese spread. Labeling the cheeses will help your guests know what they are eating. Of course, have an assortment of crackers, crostini, and fresh baguette slices as well as a bowl of small bunches of red and green grapes, walnut halves, or whole almonds. Don't forget knives or cheese slicers, and have plenty of napkins and small plates on the table. This way your guests can help themselves.

Traditional Dutch snack platter (BITTERGARNITUUR)

A *bittergarnituur* is what people order in a restaurant to go with their alcoholic drinks. The name means "accompaniments to the bitter drink of Jenever," which is Dutch gin distilled with juniper berries. While the platter varies from restaurant to restaurant, it generally consists of: small pickles called *cornichons*, salted peanuts, cheese cubes, sometimes cheese balls, crackers, sliced baguettes or dark rye bread with flavored butters or spreads, and croquette balls *(bitterballen)*.

Snacks in a dairy country like the Netherlands contain cheese, and cheese cubes and cheese balls are, of course, part of the *bittergarnituur.* The Dutch eat cheese for breakfast, lunch, and as between-meal snacks. Sometimes breaded fried cheese slices are served instead of meat or fish as the main course for dinner. Cheeses are generally named for the area where they are made, hence the names Gouda and Edam. It has been written that the charming little town of Edam closely resembled seventeenth-century New Amsterdam, now New York. The city of Gouda is known not only for its cheese, but also for locally made candles and especially for its *stroopwafels,* syrup waffles. Leyden, for which cumin cheese is named, can boast of being Holland's oldest university town (1574).

For the cheese cube portion of the *bittergarnituur,* use Gouda or Edam or one of the other tasty Dutch cheeses mentioned. Cut the cheeses into neat cubes, and poke each cube with a toothpick for easy eating. A nice touch is to use toothpicks with little Dutch flags. Alongside, serve a small dish of whole-grain mustard for dipping. In *De Zaanse Schans,* a touristy but interesting living museum north of Amsterdam, you can visit a mustard mill, where mustard seed is still ground by wind power, and where you can buy their delicious *Zaanse mosterd.* Mustard, like cheese, is named for where it is made, e.g. Groninger mustard, named for Groningen, the capital city of the province by the same name and the largest city in the northern Netherlands, and Doesburg mustard for the charming old town of Doesburg in the eastern Netherlands, near the German border. Many towns have their own mustard, a favorite condiment in the Netherlands. If you do not have access to Dutch mustard, use a whole-grain mustard.

Calf's ears (KALFSOREN)

No, this recipe is not for actual ears of calves, but for small bread slices topped with a well-seasoned veal mixture. It makes an elegant dinner or lunch dish despite its name. The original recipe can be found in the 1683 edition of *De Verstandige Kok* (*The Sensible Cook*).

FOR THE VEAL:

1 tablespoon oil

¾ pound veal stew meat cubes

½ to 1 teaspoon finely textured salt

4 tablespoons white wine or water, or more as needed

FOR THE CALF'S EARS:

2 cups finely chopped cooked veal

¼ teaspoon freshly grated nutmeg

Scant ¼ teaspoon ground mace

1 teaspoon granulated sugar

3 egg yolks

8 (½-inch thick) white bread slices (cut from firm, round dinner rolls, about 2½ inches in diameter)

3 tablespoons butter, for frying

Chopped parsley or thyme sprigs, for garnish

TO COOK THE VEAL: In a heavy frying pan over high heat, add oil and brown veal cubes on all sides. Lightly season with salt. Add 4 tablespoons of white wine or water to the pan, cover, and reduce the heat to low. Check after 15 minutes and add more liquid if necessary. Braise the meat for 45 minutes, or until tender. Finely chop the meat, making about 2 cups. Set aside.

TO PREPARE THE CALF'S EARS: In a bowl, combine chopped meat, nutmeg, mace, sugar, and yolks. Spread the meat mixture evenly and thickly over the slices of bread. In a frying pan large enough to hold 4 slices in one flat layer, heat the butter until sizzling. Place 4 slices of bread, topping side up, in the pan, and brown the bread. Then carefully flip the slices over, using tongs or two spoons, and brown the tops. Transfer to a platter, keep warm, and repeat with remaining bread slices. Serve warm, garnish with chopped parsley or thyme sprigs. Yield: 8 slices

Cheese balls (KAAS BALLETJES)

The cheese balls are a delicious addition to any snack or hors d'oeuvres tray.

8 tablespoons (1 stick) unsalted butter or cream cheese

1 cup grated Gouda cheese

2 tablespoons minced scallions or chives

2 teaspoons whole-grain mustard

Pinch cayenne pepper

3 or 4 slices whole-grain dark rye bread, crumbled

In a food processor, cream butter, cheese, scallions or chives, mustard, and cayenne, and pulse until a smooth paste forms. Cover with plastic wrap and refrigerate. Once the paste is cold, form into 1-inch balls and roll in the bread crumbs. Store in airtight containers refrigerated until ready to serve. Yield: about 20 balls.

Cheese puffs (KAASSOESJES)

Cream puffs do not always have sweet fillings. They are great filled with cheese butter or any of the other butters in this chapter.

FOR THE CHEESE FILLING:

12 tablespoons (1½ sticks) salted butter, room temperature, plus extra for garnish

1 cup finely grated aged Gouda cheese, plus extra for garnish

Cheese puffs *(Kaassoesjes)*

FOR THE DOUGH:

1 cup whole milk

6 tablespoons unsalted butter

¼ teaspoon finely textured salt

1 cup all-purpose flour

4 large eggs, room temperature

MAKE THE CHEESE FILLING: Beat butter and cheese until combined. Set aside.

MAKE THE DOUGH: Preheat oven to 400°F. In a small saucepan, bring milk, butter, and salt to a boil, then add flour all at once. Stir until a smooth paste forms. Remove from heat, and cool for 1 minute. Add eggs, one at a time, and incorporate each completely before adding the next one.

BAKE THE PUFFS: Use two small spoons to form paste into small balls. Arrange on buttered baking sheets about 1-inch apart. Bake in batches for about 15 minutes. When each batch is done, turn the oven off and open the door, but do not remove baking sheet. Let stand for about 10 minutes to allow puffs to dry a little more and crisp further. This is the trick to a perfect puff! Remove and cool on racks.

FILL THE PUFFS: Once cooled, make a small slit in each puff, open and fill with cheese butter. After filling, brush each puff on top with a little soft butter and sprinkle on some grated cheese for decoration. Yield: 30 puffs.

Croquette balls and croquettes (BITTERBALLEN EN KROKETTEN)

Croquette balls are a traditional part of the Dutch *bittergarnituur.* Larger cylindrical croquettes are often served for lunch. A standard order is "*2 croquetten met brood*"—2 croquettes with buttered bread slices—served, of course, with a dish of mustard. I get homesick thinking about it!

4 cups cold water
1¼ pound round steak, trimmed of most fat
1 small yellow onion, peeled
2 bay leaves
1 stalk celery with leaves
4 tablespoons unsalted butter
6 tablespoons all-purpose flour
1 teaspoon Worcestershire sauce
1 teaspoon finely textured salt
Freshly ground black pepper, to taste
1 egg yolk
½ cup plain bread crumbs, or more as needed
1 egg white with 1 tablespoon water, beaten
Oil, for frying

Pour water into a 2-quart saucepan, add meat, onion, 1 bay leaf, and celery. Bring to a boil uncovered, making sure it does not boil over. Skim carefully. Reduce heat, cover, and simmer for 1 to 1½ hours. Once meat is fork tender, transfer it to a cutting board. Strain, and reserve liquid, discarding bay leaf, onion, and celery. Cut the meat into ¼-inch cubes. In a medium saucepan over low heat, melt butter, then add flour, stirring to brown lightly. Whisk in 1½ cups of reserved liquid a little at a time. Once all the liquid has been added, stir the sauce and cook for 3 more minutes. Add meat cubes, Worcestershire sauce, salt, pepper, and remaining bay leaf. Simmer for 5 minutes, stirring occasionally. Stir in the egg yolk, and cook for 1 minute more. Remove from heat. Discard bay leaf. Spread this ragout on a large plate to solidify and cool. If necessary, cover with plastic wrap and refrigerate overnight. When you are ready to make the croquettes, place bread crumbs on one plate and beaten egg white on another.

TO MAKE THE CROQUETTE BALLS: Remove the meat mixture from the refrigerator, and on a clean work surface, knead it and form 18 to 20 (1½-inch) balls. Roll each ball first in the egg white, shake off any excess, and then in the bread crumbs, covering completely. At this point, the balls can be covered and refrigerated until ready to fry. Yield: 18 to 20 croquette balls

TO MAKE THE CROQUETTES:Remove the meat mixture from the refrigerator, and on a clean work surface, knead it and form 10 (3- to 3½-inch) cylinders. Roll each log in the egg white, shake off any excess, and then in the bread crumbs, coating the entire log, including the ends. At this point, the croquettes can be covered and refrigerated until ready to fry.

TO FRY: In a large pot, heat about 4 inches of oil to 350°F, or in a deep fryer, carefully fry 4 or 5 croquette balls or 2 or 3 croquettes at a time, until deep brown. Transfer to paper towels to drain. Serve with whole-grain mustard. Yield: 10 croquettes.

Croquette balls *(Bitterballen)*

Deviled eggs (GEVULDE EIEREN)

Dutch deviled eggs are traditionally made with mustard and with less mayonnaise than American versions.

6 hard-boiled eggs
2 tablespoons good-quality mayonnaise
1 tablespoon whole-grain Dutch mustard
Salt and freshly ground black pepper
Minced scallion or chives, mixed with minced parsley, for garnish

Cut eggs in half, remove yolks, and sprinkle whites lightly with salt. Arrange egg whites on a platter. In a small bowl, mash yolks with a fork, while adding in mayonnaise, mustard and a few grindings of pepper. Spoon yolks into egg halves and press with fork to make a neat filling. Garnish each with a sprinkling of herbs Yield: 12 egg halves.

Flavored savory butters

Flavored butters are generally served with thin baguette slices, or if you prefer, small whole-grain bread slices.

Cheese butter (KAASBOTER)

8 tablespoons (1 stick) salted butter, room temperature

1 cup grated aged cheese, preferably Gouda or Old Amsterdam

Pinch ground white pepper

In an electric mixer, beat all ingredients until thoroughly combined. On a piece of plastic wrap, shape the cheese butter into a roll, cover, and refrigerate for at least 1 hour before serving. To serve, cut into neat round slices.

Herb butter (KRUIDENBOTER)

8 tablespoons (1 stick) salted butter, room temperature

4 tablespoons of a mixture of minced chives or scallions and minced parsley

Pinch ground white pepper

In an electric mixer, beat all ingredients until thoroughly combined. On a piece of plastic wrap, shape the herb butter into a roll, cover, and refrigerate for at least 1 hour before serving. To serve, cut into neat round slices.

Shrimp butter (GARNALENBOTER)

8 tablespoons (1 stick) salted butter, room temperature

4 tablespoons finely minced cooked shrimp

⅛ teaspoon hot sauce (use your favorite brand)

In an electric mixer, beat all ingredients until thoroughly combined. On a piece of plastic wrap, shape the shrimp butter into a roll, cover, and refrigerate for at least 1 hour before serving. To serve, cut into neat round slices.

Ham and asparagus rolls (HAM EN ASPERGE ROLLETJES)

These make a great hors d'oeuvre or a nice first course when served with a small salad.

1 hard-boiled egg, mashed with a fork

½ cup good-quality mayonnaise

2 tablespoons chopped capers

2 scant tablespoons finely chopped sweet-sour pickles

1 tablespoon minced parsley

1 tablespoon minced scallions

Salt and freshly ground black pepper, to taste

8 thin ham slices (but not too thin)

16 to 24 asparagus spears, depending on thickness, steamed

In a small bowl, combine first 6 ingredients. Taste, and add salt and pepper, as needed. Spread sauce on each ham slice, place 2 or 3 asparagus spears in the middle, and roll up. Cut across in half. Yield: 16 rolls.

Ham puffs (HAMSOESJES)

These small cream puffs are delicious with this savory ham filling.

FOR THE HAM SALAD FILLING:

1 cup minced ham

3 tablespoons minced celery stalk with some leaves

1 minced gherkin (about 1 tablespoon)

2 to 3 tablespoons mayonnaise mixed with 1 teaspoon whole-grain mustard

FOR THE DOUGH:

1 cup whole milk

6 tablespoons unsalted butter, plus extra for garnish

¼ teaspoon finely textured salt

1 cup all-purpose flour

4 large eggs, room temperature

Minced parsley, for garnish

Aged Gouda cheese, for garnish

MAKE THE HAM SALAD: In a small bowl, combine all ingredients well. Set aside.

MAKE THE DOUGH: Preheat oven to 400°F. In a small saucepan, bring milk, butter, and salt to a boil, then add flour all at once. Stir until a smooth paste forms. Remove from heat, and cool for 1 minute. Add eggs, one at a time, and incorporate each completely before adding the next one.

BAKE THE PUFFS: Use two small spoons to form paste into small balls. Arrange on buttered baking sheets about 1-inch apart. Bake in batches for about 15 minutes. When each batch is done, turn oven off, open door but do not remove baking sheet. Let stand for about 10 minutes to allow puffs to dry a little more and crisp further. This is the trick to a perfect puff! Remove and cool on racks.

FILL THE PUFFS: Once cooled, make a small slit in each puff, open and fill with ham salad. After filling, brush each puff on top with a little soft butter and sprinkle on some grated cheese for decoration. Yield: 30 puffs.

Sausage rolls (SAUCIJZENBROODJES)

Again, here is a recipe that makes a nice hors d'oeuvre or a good starter when served with a small salad. *Saucijzenbroodjes* are for sale in the many snack shops that dot Dutch cities.

1 pound pork sausage (I use Jimmy Dean brand)

2 sheets frozen puff pastry (I use Pepperidge Farm brand), thawed

1 egg beaten lightly, for egg wash

Preheat oven to 400°F. On a large cutting board, roll sausage meat into 24 (1-inch) balls, then roll them into 2-inch sausage logs. On a lightly floured work surface, unroll each puff pastry sheet. Cut each sheet into 3 pieces along the folds. Then cut each of these strips into 4 (2½x3-inch) pieces, for a total of 24 pieces. Place 1 dough piece with the short side toward you, top with a sausage log, then roll and pinch the ends. Repeat. Place rolls on buttered baking sheets, seam side down. Brush the tops with egg wash. Bake in batches for 15 to 20 minutes, or until golden and the filling is fully cooked. Cut into one to make sure! Yield: 24 sausage rolls.

Shrimp salad in plum tomatoes

(GEVULDE TOMAATJES MET GARNALENSLA)

These versatile stuffed tomatoes can be served as a snack, a starter paired with a green salad, or one of the items that surround the mixed cooked vegetable salad (see recipe in chapter 7).

6 plum tomatoes, cut in half lengthwise

Finely textured salt, divided

½ pound medium cooked shrimp, cut into small pieces

1 heaping tablespoon finely chopped sweet-sour pickles

1 hard-boiled egg, chopped

2 to 3 tablespoons good-quality mayonnaise

2 teaspoons fresh lemon juice

Freshly ground black pepper, to taste

Minced parsley, for garnish

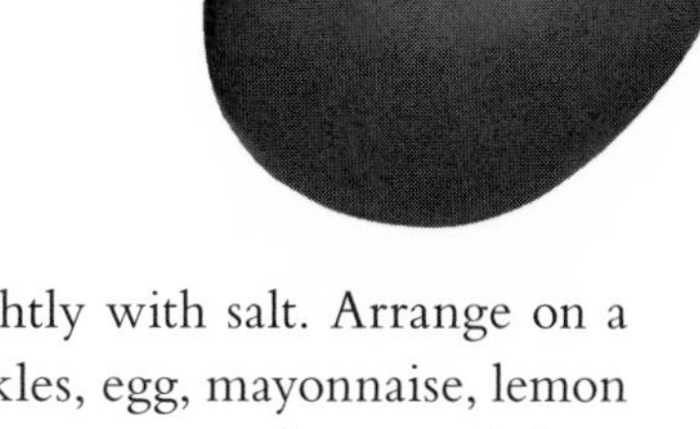

Hollow out the tomato halves and sprinkle the inside lightly with salt. Arrange on a platter, and set aside. In a small bowl, combine shrimp, pickles, egg, mayonnaise, lemon juice, and season with salt and pepper. Spoon the mixture into prepared tomato halves. Top with a pinch of parsley. Yield: 12 tomato halves.

Smoked mackerel paté (GEROOKTE MAKREEL PATÉ)

American supermarkets carry the usual smoked salmon as well as mackerel fillets, which is a favorite fish in the Netherlands and is particularly good in this spread for crackers.

8 ounces smoked mackerel, finely chopped

⅓ cup light mayonnaise

⅓ cup reduced fat sour cream

1 tablespoon minced scallions

2 heaping tablespoons tiny capers, or large chopped capers, plus extra for garnish

Coarsely ground fresh black pepper

Sea salt, as needed

In a small serving bowl, combine all ingredients except for salt. Taste, and add salt only if necessary. Smooth the top with a knife, and garnish with a few extra capers. Serve with crackers.

10

Recipes for Festive Homemade Drinks

Anise milk *(Anijsmelk)*
Bishop *(Bisschopwijn)*
Brandied apricots *(Boerenmeisjes)*
Brandied raisins *(Boerenjongens)*
Dutch eggnog *(Advokaat)*
Hippocras
Hot chocolate for children *(Chocolademelk)*
Hot spiced chocolate, my way
Hot double devil
Norman's dream
Spiced milk *(Slemp)*

Anise milk (ANIJSMELK)

In a dairy country like the Netherlands, it is logical to find milk- and egg-based drinks. Anise milk was, and still is, a winter favorite, particularly at ice-skating time, when convenient "cake and drink" stands, called *koek en zopie,* appear. Anise milk as well as chocolate milk are traditional drinks for children during Saint Nicholas festivities.

4 cups whole milk
1 tablespoon anise seed, crushed and tied in cheesecloth, or use a "tea egg"
¼ cup granulated sugar
2 teaspoons cornstarch, optional

In a saucepan, combine milk, sugar, and anise seed bundle, and bring to a boil slowly. Allow to simmer for 30 minutes over low heat. Remove anise seed, and squeeze the packet over the pan to catch all the flavored juice. In a small bowl, combine cornstarch and 1 tablespoon of warm milk. Then stir the cornstarch mixture into the saucepan of flavored milk to thicken, if desired. Stir, pour into mugs, and serve warm. Serves 4.

Bishop (BISSCHOPWIJN)

Bishop is a lovely spiced wine that is the traditional drink for *Sinterklaasavond,* the December 5 Dutch gift-giving event.

4 cups water

1 teaspoon ground mace or 2 blades whole mace

4 (3-inch) cinnamon sticks

2 navel oranges, washed thoroughly and studded with 10 cloves each

4 bottles red wine, such as Merlot

Granulated sugar, to taste

Navel orange slices, for garnish

In a saucepan, bring water and spices to a boil, add oranges, and simmer on low heat for 1 hour. Cut oranges in half and squeeze juice into spice mixture. Strain mixture through a sieve. In a large pan, combine strained liquid and wine. Reheat, but do not boil. Add sugar, to taste. This mulled wine is not meant to be very sweet, add just enough sugar to accentuate the spiced, fruity taste. Perhaps offer more sugar in a bowl separately. Pour into clear glass mugs or punch cups to show off the beautiful ruby color of the wine. Garnish each serving with a half slice of orange, if desired.

Brandied apricots (BOERENMEISJES)

This traditional Dutch drink is served in a small glass with a tiny spoon for scooping up the apricot pieces. I still have a box full of engraved silver spoons that my great grandmother used for this specific purpose. *Boerenmeisjes* means farmers' girls in Dutch, and its sister drink, *Boerenjongens,* brandied raisins, means farmers' boys in Dutch. These specialty drinks came from the Groningen region, and were favorite drinks with the farmers, which may explain the names. Note: Recipe takes 2 days to complete, at least 2 months to macerate (the longer it stands, the better it gets), and you will need 1 (1½- to 2-quart) glass jar and lid.

1½ cups dried apricots, diced small

2 cups granulated sugar

2½ cups water

2-inch piece thin lemon peel

750-milliliter bottle (1 fifth) good-quality French brandy

In a large saucepan, heat water and sugar until sugar dissolves. Add apricots and lemon peel and simmer until apricots are softened. Make sure there is enough water to cover the apricot pieces. Remove from heat, cool, and refrigerate for 2 days. With a slotted

Brandied apricots *(Boerenmeisjes)*

spoon place the apricot pieces in a 1½- to 2-quart sterilized jar. Discard the lemon peel. Cook down the sugar mixture until syrupy, about 10 minutes. Cool and pour in the jar. Once the apricot mixture has completely cooled, add the brandy and close the jar airtight. Put away in a cool, dark place for at least 2 months before serving. This brandy improves with age. Serve the traditional way in small glasses with a little spoon or use as a topping for custard or vanilla ice cream. Yield: about 1½ quarts.

Brandied raisins (BOERENJONGENS)

In New Netherland, the seventeenth-century Dutch colony in North America, this drink was traditionally served for any festive occasion. It was presented in a communal, silver two-handled "brandy wine bowl," which was passed along from one person to another. Each person used their own spoon to scoop out the macerated fruit. Some of these beautiful bowls have found their way into the Albany Institute of History & Art, and New York Historical Society, in New York City. Note: Recipe needs 2 months to macerate, and you will need 1 (1½- to 2-quart) glass jar and lid.

2 cups water

2 cups granulated sugar

2 (3-inch) cinnamon sticks

1 pound golden raisins

750-milliliter bottle (1 fifth) good-quality French brandy

In a large saucepan, heat water and sugar until sugar dissolves. Add cinnamon and raisins, and simmer for 10 minutes. Make sure there is enough water to cover the raisins. First, with a slotted spoon, place raisins in the sterilized jar. Gently boil sugar mixture until syrupy, about 10 minutes. Cool and pour in the jar. Once the raisin mixture has completely cooled, fill the jar with brandy. Seal the jar tightly and store in a cool, dark place for 2 months before serving. The brandy will improve with age. Serve in small glasses with a little spoon for scooping up the raisins. Yield: about 1½ quarts.

Dutch Eggnog (ADVOKAAT)

Dutch eggnog is an alcoholic drink and much thicker than the American version. It is considered a "ladies drink" that is served in small liqueur glasses with a tiny spoon. This recipe makes at least 12 generous servings, but can be doubled as needed. Note: You will need 1 (8- or 16-ounce) glass jar and lid.

4 eggs

1 cup granulated sugar

½ vanilla bean, seeds scraped

1 cup good-quality French brandy

4 tablespoons hot water

In an electric mixer, combine eggs, sugar, and vanilla bean seeds, beating at high speed until thick, about 3 minutes. Reduce speed to slow, add the brandy and hot water a little at a time. Pour egg mixture either into a bowl placed over boiling water, making sure bowl does not touch water or the top pan of a double boiler. Whisk until thick and mounds slightly when dropped off a spoon. *Be very careful. If cooked too long the mixture will curdle.* Transfer to a sterilized jar, and cool. Seal tightly and store in the refrigerator until ready to use. Serve in small glasses with little spoons, and for an-over-the-top treat, add a dollop of sweetened whipped cream. Yield: 12 servings, or more depending on size.

Hippocras

Hippocras, a sweetened spiced wine, is a drink with a long history. Recipes for it appear in both Dutch and English cookbooks, and mentions of it being served at elaborate banquets go back to the Middle Ages. It can be made with either red or white dry wine. This recipe, created by food historian Stephen Schmidt, is based on one by Robert May in *Accomplished Cook (1660–1685)*. I think his is the best version of this drink. I am sure you will find it as irresistible as my friends do when I serve it as the festive end of my annual Christmas tea (see chapter 11). Note: Wine needs to steep for 24 hours, and you will need a 2-quart or larger glass jar with lid.

8 (3-inch) cinnamon sticks
4 large or 6 small nutmegs
4 teaspoons whole cloves
7 whole peppercorns
8 cups (2 quarts) pleasant, neutral-tasting wine (such as Pinot Grigio, but not Chardonnay, which is too oaky)
⅓ cup fresh ginger, peeled and chopped
1½ teaspoons dried rosemary
4 cups granulated sugar

Combine cinnamon, nutmegs, cloves, and peppercorns in a sturdy, zipper-top plastic bag and whack with a small heavy skillet or hammer until coarsely crushed. Pour the wine in a large sterilized jar and stir in the crushed spices, ginger, and rosemary. Cover, and let steep for 24 hours (but no longer). Strain through a fine-mesh sieve, shaking the spice debris in order to keep as much wine as possible. Pour 1 cup of wine through a coffee filter. Change the filter, repeat 1 cup at a time, until all the wine is filtered and clear. Mix the wine with 4 cups sugar and let stand until the sugar completely dissolves, which will take several hours. The wine will keep indefinitely in the refrigerator. Yield: about 2½ quarts.

Hot chocolate for children (CHOCOLADEMELK)

A warm and delicious hot chocolate that can only be made better with big dollops of whipped cream!

4 cups (1 quart) whole milk
½ cup cocoa powder (I use Droste brand)
¼ cup granulated sugar
Sweetened whipped cream, optional

In a small bowl, combine ½ cup milk, cocoa powder, and sugar, stirring to make a smooth sauce. In a saucepan, bring the remaining milk to a boil, then stir in cocoa-milk mixture. Reduce heat to low, and softly boil the chocolate milk for a 3 or 4 minutes. Pour into mugs and serve with whipped cream if desired. Yield: 4 (8-ounce) servings.

Hot spiced chocolate, my way

My adult version was inspired by a collaborative project on the use of chocolate in America that resulted in the book, *Chocolate, History, Culture, and Heritage* (Wiley, 2009). This recipe is quite high in caffeine and may keep you up at night, but it is delicious.

4 squares unsweetened baking chocolate, cut into quarters

½ teaspoon ground cinnamon

⅛ teaspoon cayenne powder, or more as desired

¼ teaspoon ground ginger

3 to 4 teaspoons granulated sugar, or more as desired

2 cups boiling water

½ teaspoon pure vanilla extract

2 cups boiling whole milk or half-and-half

Sweetened whipped cream, optional

In a food processor fitted with a metal blade, pulse chocolate until it resembles fine granules. In a 1- or 2-quart saucepan. mix chocolate, cinnamon, cayenne, ginger, and sugar. Slowly pour boiling water over dry ingredients, whisking until chocolate dissolves. Add vanilla and milk or half and half, and continue whisking until well incorporated. Pour into mugs, serve with whipped cream if desired. Yield: 8 (4-ounce) cups.

Hot double devil

For my book about chocolate, *Festive Chocolate*, my friend Andrea Candee helped me create some delicious alcoholic drinks using *Theobroma cacao*, the botanical name for cocoa, which means appropriately "food of the gods." She devised this warming potion for a devilishly cold December night. What a way to wrap up an evening party or chilly winter's night by a cozy fire. Note: Recipe can easily be multiplied.

¾ ounce almond liqueur

¾ ounce chocolate liqueur

¾ ounce coffee liqueur

6 ounces hot coffee

Sweetened whipped cream, optional

In a glass, combine the liqueurs. Pour the coffee into a mug and stir in the liqueurs. Top with cream, if desired. Yield: 1 serving.

Norman's Dream

This simple ice cream drink always seems festive and is the perfect ending to a comforting December meal. I named it after our friend, the late Dr. Norman J. Larson who was known for his homemade curaçao. Serve this as an easy dessert with cookies, perhaps the chocolate almond crunchies from chapter 5 (see recipe, page 65). Note: Recipe can easily be multiplied.

1½ ounces curaçao (or other orange-flavored liqueur)

1 generous scoop chocolate ice cream

Chocolate shavings, grated orange zest, sweetened whipped cream, optional garnishes

In a blender, combine curaçao and ice cream until just smooth. Pour into a wide-mouthed margarita or similar glass and garnish as desired. The drink is quite good without the trimmings, too. Drink can be made ahead; just keep in blender jar in the freezer up to 2 hours. Stir before serving. Yield: 1 serving.

Spiced milk (SLEMP)

My mother would tell me stories about drinking *slemp*, a spiced milk drink. Like anise milk, it was served in little stands along the frozen rivers and canals when the winters were cold and people were ice skating. It was also served at home as a special treat on a night when parents and children played board games. Does anyone play board games anymore?

4 cups (1 quart) whole milk

2 (3-inch) cinnamon sticks

12 whole cloves

¼ cup granulated sugar, or more to taste

Pinch saffron, if available and if desired

3 black tea bags

Rinse a medium saucepan with water, then add milk and bring to a boil. Tie the cinnamon, cloves, and saffron, if desired, in a piece of cheesecloth. Stir in sugar, and drop cheesecloth bundle and tea bags into the boiling milk. Reduce heat, and simmer for 45 minutes. Pour into mugs and serve. Yield: 4 (1-cup) servings.

Presents, Poems, Decorations, Menus, and Recipes

Apricot coconut squares *(Abrikozentaart met kokos)*

Cheese tart with almonds *(Kaas taert)*

Cheese and mustard pretzels *(Broodkrakelingen met kaas en mosterd)*

Chicken and almond sandwiches *(Kip met amandel sandwiches)*

Chicken and mushrooms ragout in puff pastry shells *(Kipragout in vol-au-vents)*

Chip's cucumber sandwiches *(Komkommer sandwiches)*

Cod with mustard sauce *(Kabeljauw met mosterdsaus)*

Coleslaw with hot butter dressing *(Koolsla)*

Farmer's omelet *(Boerenomelet)*

French toast, the Dutch way *(Wentelteefjes)*

Hazelnut tart *(Hazelnoottaart)*

Indonesian cucumber salad *(Atjar ketimun)*

Kippered herring sandwiches *(Gerookte haring sandwiches)*

Mother's pudding

Mushroom fricassee with orange

Mushroom quiche without a crust *(Paddestoelentaart zonder korst)*

Mustard soup (*Mosterdsoep*)

Orange-hazelnut crusted chicken breasts *(Kippeborst met hazelnootkorst)*

Rice pudding with wine and currants *(Rijstebrij met krenten)*

Star anise stew *(Semur daging (Indonesian))*

Stuffed tomatoes with lentil salad *(Gevulde tomaten met linzensla)*

Sunday cabbage *(Zondagse kool)*

Vegetable soup with small meatballs *(Groentesoep met balletjes)*

Presents

The Netherlands' largest supermarket chain Albert Heijn, which is so big it owns the American chain of Stop & Shop stores, publishes a free magazine called *Allerhande,* which means a little of everything. Their 2012 holiday issue gave some advice on gifts for *Sinterklaas.* While presents for the main Dutch gift-giving occasion are generally small, it is what you do with them, how ingeniously you disguise them, and how apropos your poem is to the gift or the giver that counts, not the value of the gift. Some examples from the magazine under the heading of "presents that are always good:" For mother, a notepad; for a friend, a thick stack of magazines; for a child, rubber letter stamps with ink pad; for grandparents, tickets for the zoo so they can go together with their grandchildren; for the sister who loves sweets, some of the *Sinterklaas* specialties; for everybody, a photo present such as a calendar, mug, or t-shirt. As you can see, it is not quite the abundance American magazines would suggest. Here are some other ideas for gifts that are always happily received and require little shopping: gift cards, magazine subscriptions, museum memberships, theater or concert tickets, and restaurant gift certificates.

Ornaments are wonderful last-minute presents. For the cook, there are various food-shaped decorations—fruits such as strawberries, apples, pears, banana, watermelon slices, ears of corn, pickles—and kitchen gadgets such as teapots, knives, and forks, and I've even seen a whole miniature dinner service. For men there are boats, cars, airplanes, and even golf clubs. The choice is truly endless.

In the Introduction, I wrote about the inventive way of wrapping and disguising a present called "surprise," pronounced the French way, "surpreese." It is an integral part of the celebration and also a way to make the present anonymous. Remember, all presents come from *Sinterklaas.* Check the mail order and website list at the end of the book for a Dutch website with great ideas for creative wraps that will lead to great poems!

Poems

The pedagogical aspect of Saint Nicholas' giving is still retained by making this an occasion where one may—in rhyme form—tell about the recipient's foibles. An irritating or funny habit may be the subject of a long poem, and the author will end it by hoping the habit will be corrected next year, or else.... To some, the rhyming seems a daunting task, while others make light of it. We were fortunate when our son-in-law, Jason Harris, immediately grasped the concept at his first celebration and wrote a poem for a liquid soap dispenser that has become a classic in our family:

> Dirty little fingers can mess up the house.
> Dirty little fingers, like feetprints from a mouse.
> Dirty little fingers leaving spots on the walls.
> Leaving marks on the banister, and streaks in the halls
> With dirty little fingers, important papers get a smudge
> After eating special treats of rich chocolate fudge.
> Now there is only one solution to this dirty little sin

That is to have one of these near every room you're in
Then your dirty little fingers can be clean and pure and nice
And you can leave the nasty smudging to those rude and thoughtless mice.
Saint Nicholas

In our house, we generally start the celebration at about 6 p.m., but reading, and often re-reading, each poem, debating who is the best poet of the year, and unwrapping the present and passing it around, takes time. So it is usually quite late before all is finished, and we jointly call out: "Thank you, Saint Nicholas!"

Decorations

For the Saint Nicholas celebration there are no special decorations. The emphasis is on the inventively wrapped or disguised presents.

For Christmas, however, people like to bring in lots of greens, candles, glittering decorations, and a tree—though not as large as the American Christmas trees, because, in general, Dutch houses are smaller. In fact, American Christmas decorations, inside or outside, are also far more lavish than the Dutch ones.

In my hometown of Zeist, we have a special decoration in the form of a paper Moravian star that hangs in many houses in town starting on the first day of Advent and ending on Epiphany, or January 6. The Moravian community was founded in Zeist on May 12, 1746, and its community's buildings flank the Zeist castle on either side—the sister square, *Zusterplein,* and the brother square, *Broederplein.* The elementary school I attended was in the *Zusterplein* since I lived so close to it, and it was there where I learned the Moravian customs. When I came to America, I even brought a Moravian star with me. Each year, on the first Sunday of Advent, my husband puts together our star, inserts a small electric light, and hangs it in our front window to proclaim that Christmas is near.

When I grew up, Advent Sunday marked the beginning of Christmas preparations. My mother's table setting for Christmas dinner was beautiful, and it started with the ironing of the red ribbons she saved from year to year. First, she covered the table with a gleaming white damask cloth, also properly ironed, of course, and then ran a long strip of the freshly pressed red ribbon down the middle of the table and more across each end, about a foot in from the edge. The place settings also included crystal or silver knife rests, which we used in those days, and Mother's best glasses. She would make a centerpiece of greens, little red Christmas tulips (unknown in the United States) and lots of candles. Pinecones were used as place card holders, and the children would write and decorate the menus. Those menus, I realized later, were a clever ploy to keep us kids busy while Mother was in the kitchen preparing the various dishes. The ploy still works, of course, and it gives children a sense of pride to be part of the preparation for this big occasion.

Other table decorating ideas include small goodie bags tied with ribbons and nametags that also double as place markers. The goodie bags can be filled with some of the home-made chocolates from chapter 5, or simply with store-bought chocolate coins. If possible, attach a recipe card, or a special ingredient, if appropriate. A chocolate lollipop or some candy canes tied together also serve as place markers. Be creative with wrapping—there are so many possibilities, and local party stores are good resources. Another festive and longer-lasting goodie-bag idea is to give your guests a mesh bag with paperwhite bulbs, which when planted indoors bring a bowl of scented seasonal cheer.

Try this decorating idea—make your dessert, perhaps a compote or a small trifle, even more celebratory by placing it in the middle of a plate and surrounding it with Christmas cookies, candies, and a red rose or a bit of green to make an extra festive presentation.

Menus

The following menus are not meant for the actual holidays, but rather for the days in between when you might have guests and want meals to be festive "without overdoing" it. Where necessary, recipes are provided and indicated by an (r) symbol.

FESTIVE DECEMBER LUNCHES

The lunch menus all contain some very typical Dutch dishes. Vegetable soup with small meatballs in the first menu was the quintessential soup for Sunday dinner when I grew up. Ragout or white sauce with chicken and mushrooms in puff pastry is also old-fashioned, but people always enjoy it when it is properly made. The added benefit is both the shells and ragout can be prepared ahead, as can the soup, and the hazelnut tart is even better the second day!

Lunch menu I

(r)**Vegetable soup with small meatballs** *(Groentesoep met balletjes)*

(r)**Chicken and mushroom ragout in puff pastry shells** (*Kip ragout in vol-au-vents)*

Green salad with vinaigrette dressing

(r)Hazelnut tart *(Hazelnoottaart)*

Vegetable soup with small meatballs (GROENTESOEP MET BALLETJES)

FOR THE HOMEMADE BROTH:

12 cups (3 quarts) water

3 pounds beef soup bones

1 marrow bone

4 stalks celery

1 yellow onion, quartered

5 whole cloves

10 whole peppercorns, crushed

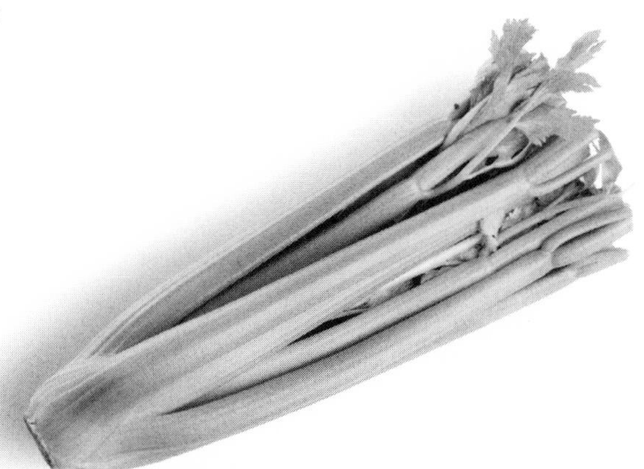

FOR THE MEATBALLS:

1 thick slice bread, whole grain or white, crusts removed

3 tablespoons whole milk

½ pound ground beef

½ teaspoon finely textured salt and a few grinds of black pepper

⅛ teaspoon ground nutmeg

FOR THE SOUP:

12 cups (3 quarts) homemade or store-bought beef broth

½ to 1 cup finely diced carrots

½ to 1 cup julienned cabbage

½ to 1 cup diced green beans

½ to 1 cup finely diced celery, including leaves

½ cup finely minced parsley

½ to 1 cup cauliflower, broken into tiny florets or pieces

½ to 1 cup green peas

½ cup finely diced tomatoes (not too much they will dominate the flavor of the soup)

4 ounces vermicelli, broken into 3 or 4 pieces

Salt and freshly ground black pepper, to taste

MAKE THE BROTH: In a large stockpot, bring all ingredients to a boil. Skim. Simmer for 2 or 3 hours. Cool. Strain and discard solids. Refrigerate overnight. The next day remove and discard hardened fat. Return broth to a clean pot.

MAKE THE MEATBALLS: Soak bread in milk and combine with ground beef and seasonings. Roll into balls the size of marbles.

MAKE THE SOUP: Bring the homemade or store-bought broth to a boil. Carefully drop in meatballs and all vegetables. Cook over medium heat for 20 minutes, add broken pasta and cook 10 minutes more. Taste, add salt and pepper as necessary. Yield: 12 servings

Chicken and mushroom ragout in puff pastry shells

(KIPRAGOUT IN VOL-AU-VENTS)

- 1 tablespoon vegetable oil
- 10 ounces sliced mushrooms, rinsed and dried
- 2 tablespoons chopped scallions
- 2 tablespoons chopped parsley
- 6 tablespoons unsalted butter
- 6 tablespoons all-purpose flour
- 1½ cups whole milk
- 1½ cups cooked chicken or leftover turkey, diced
- ½ teaspoon finely textured salt
- ¼ teaspoon freshly ground white pepper
- 6 (1 package) puff pastry shells, baked according to manufacturer's instructions

Heat the oil in a frying pan over medium heat and sauté mushrooms, scallions, and parsley, stirring until mushrooms are browned on both sides. Remove and set aside. In a saucepan, melt butter, then add flour, whisking until combined. Reduce heat, slowly add milk and whisk to make a smooth sauce. Continue cooking for 2 minutes to remove the raw starch taste. To the sauce, add mushrooms with any liquid, and chicken, stir to combine. Season with salt and pepper. When ready to serve, spoon ragout into pastry shells and top each with a little pastry round. Yield: 6 servings

Hazelnut tart (HAZELNOOTTAART)

- ½ cup whole hazelnuts
- 2 cups all-purpose flour
- ⅓ cup firmly packed dark brown sugar

11 tablespoons unsalted butter

¼ teaspoon finely textured salt

2 egg yolks

½ cup whole hazelnuts, or more as desired, for topping

½ cup confectioners' sugar

2 tablespoons Frangelico or other hazelnut liqueur

Preheat oven to 350°F. In a food processor fitted with a metal blade, grind hazelnuts to a fine powder. Add flour and sugar. Process briefly to combine, then add butter, salt, and egg yolks, and continue to process until a cohesive dough forms. Press dough into a buttered 9-inch pie plate or a 9-inch tart pan. Smooth the top to make the tart flat. Press the hazelnuts into the top of the tart in a close spoke pattern, so that when sliced, each wedge will get a row of hazelnuts. Bake for about 30 to 35 minutes, until light brown and done. Combine confectioners' sugar and liqueur and brush onto the warm tart, making sure to brush away any glaze puddles and make the glaze smooth over the top of the tart. Cool and remove from pan. Place on a footed cake stand. To serve: cut into thin wedges. Yield: at least 12 servings.

Lunch menu II

In this second menu, you can start with the tomatoes as a first course, or you can serve the tomatoes, salad, quiche, bread, and butter all at the same time. The quiche without a crust is based on a recipe from a rare book on mushrooms by Franciscus van Sterbeeck (1668). The compote for dessert can be made from frozen or canned fruit, or both—just combine and simply heat together. Stir in a teaspoon of lemon or orange zest for fresh flavor. Serve hot or cold.

(r)**Stuffed tomatoes with lentil salad** *(Gevulde tomaatjes met linzensla)*

(r)**Mushroom quiche without a crust** *(Paddestoelentaart zonder korst)*

Green salad with cucumber, radish, and minced scallions

Bread and butter

Custard or ice cream with fruit compote

Stuffed tomatoes with lentil salad

(GEVULDE TOMATEN MET LINZENSLA)

1 cup lentils (use your favorite)

4 cups water

3 to 4 tablespoons vinaigrette dressing (use your favorite)

2 tablespoons minced scallions

¼ cup slivered almonds

3 large plum tomatoes, cut in half lengthwise, hollowed out and lightly salted

In a large pot over medium heat cook lentils in the water for 15 to 20 minutes. After 15 minutes check often for doneness. Lentils should be soft, but not mushy. Drain, add 2 tablespoons of the vinaigrette and cool. When cooled, stir in the minced scallions and almonds and more vinaigrette if necessary, but do not make the mixture too moist. Place tomato halves on a platter and heap lentil mixture into them. Yield: 6 servings.

Mushroom quiche without a crust

(PADDESTOELENTAART ZONDER KORST)

10 ounces white mushrooms, wiped clean

1 clove garlic, minced

¼ teaspoon freshly ground black pepper

¼ teaspoon finely textured salt

¼ teaspoon dried marjoram

1 cup grated Gouda or Old Amsterdam cheese

⅓ cup whole milk

3 eggs

Preheat oven to 375°F. Reserve mushroom caps and chop stems. In a large bowl, combine mushroom stems, garlic, seasonings, and cheese. In a small bowl, lightly beat together milk and eggs; pour into mushroom stems and combine. Taste the cheese, and if it does not seem too salty, add a little more salt to the egg mixture. Place mushroom caps, open side up, in an even layer in a 9-inch pie plate. Pour egg mixture over caps, and bake for 10 minutes at 375°F. Then reduce heat to 325°F and bake for another 30 minutes, or until egg mixture sets. Cut into wedges and serve with a salad. Serves 4 to 6.

Lunch menu III

In this third menu, I give you two choices for the main cheese dishes—one a beautiful cheese tart, the other delicious cheese and mustard pretzels.

Mixed green salad

(r)**Cheese tart with almonds** *(kaas taert)* **OR**

(r)**Cheese and mustard pretzels, (***Broodkrakelingen met kaas en mosterd),* **served with ham and/or cheese**

Fruit salad with cream and cookies (from chapter 6)

Cheese tart with almonds (KAAS TAERT)

FOR THE CRUST:

2 cups all-purpose flour

11 tablespoons cold unsalted butter, cut into pats

2 egg yolks, lightly beaten with a fork

1¼ teaspoons finely textured salt

FOR THE FILLING:

1 pound young Gouda cheese

¼ cup whole wheat flour

4 eggs

2 tablespoons salted butter, melted and cooled

About 40-41 whole natural unblanched almonds

MAKE THE CRUST: Preheat oven to 375°F. In a food processor fitted with a metal blade, combine flour, butter, egg yolks, and salt. Process just until a cohesive dough forms. Press the dough on the bottom and 1¼ inches up the sides of a lightly buttered 9-inch springform pan. Run your thumb around the rim to even it.

MAKE THE FILLING: Cube cheese and pulse it and flour in a food processor fitted with a metal blade until cheese is finely chopped. Alternatively, grate cheese on the shredding plate of a box grater, then toss with the flour until the shreds are separated. In an electric mixer, whip eggs until frothy, add cheese-flour mixture and butter, and beat until smooth. Spoon filling into crust, and carefully smooth the top and decorate with a circle of almonds along the rim. Neatly place three almonds in the center. Bake for 45 to 50 minutes, or until the filling is firm and light gold. Do not overbake; it will make the filling rubbery. Serve warm or at room temperature. This "taert" can be made a few hours ahead. Yield: 1 tart, at least 12 servings, depending on size.

Cheese and mustard bread pretzels

(BROODKRAKELINGEN MET KAAS EN MOSTERD)

Over the years, I have taught many children's cooking classes, and my recipe for whole-wheat pretzels has always been a hit. This recipe is my adult version with cheese and mustard added. These pretzels will make a great lunch, perhaps sliced in half, buttered, filled with ham or a thick slice of Gouda, and accompanied by a nice cold beer. Heineken anyone? I have served these also to happy cheers at numerous sporting event parties.

2 cups whole-wheat flour

2 cups all-purpose flour

1 package active dry yeast

1 teaspoon finely textured salt

3 tablespoons oil

1 tablespoon honey

2 tablespoons coarse mustard (I use Kosciusko, if no Dutch mustard is available)

1⅓ cups hot water (120°F to 130°F)

1 egg, beaten with a fork

1 cup packed finely grated aged Gouda cheese

In a medium bowl, combine both flours, and set aside. In an electric mixer fitted with a dough paddle, combine 1½ cups of the flour mixture, yeast, salt, oil, honey, mustard, and water, and beat until smooth, adding more flour from the bowl to make a dough that is not sticky. You will probably use almost all of the remaining flour mixture. On a clean lightly floured work surface, knead the dough for 5 minutes. Cut dough into 12 pieces and roll each piece into a rope 15 inches long. Brush with egg. Spoon some grated cheese on the work surface, and roll each rope in the cheese to coat. Shape into a pretzel. Place on buttered baking sheets. Let pretzels rise for 40 minutes in a warm place. Re-shape as needed. Preheat oven to 425°F. Bake for 15 minutes, or until they are nicely browned and when a toothpick inserted comes out clean.

FESTIVE DECEMBER DINNERS

The first menu takes into account the popularity of Indonesian food in the Netherlands. When Indonesia became independent after World War II, many people repatriated to the Netherlands, and Indonesian restaurants seemingly sprouted up everywhere. I find this little menu a terrific choice for the time between Christmas and New Year's when everyone is looking for something spicy and different from the rich and heavy foods of the holidays. Serve the rice with a side dish of roasted peanuts to be sprinkled on for a satisfying crunch. If you feel you need a first course, just serve a salad with peanut dressing, now commercially available. Flavor the steamed green beans with freshly grated nutmeg. The hot pepper paste can be found in Asian specialty stores. Use it sparingly as it is quite hot. For fried bananas, a recipe is hardly needed. Use yellow bananas that are ripe, but not overripe. Use one per person. Peel, slice them lengthwise, and cut in half across. In a large frying pan, heat enough butter to amply coat the bottom and fry the bananas until light brown on both sides, dust them with cinnamon and serve them hot over coconut or vanilla ice cream.

Dinner menu I

(r)**Star anise stew** *(Semur daging (Indonesian))*

Rice with peanuts

Steamed green beans with nutmeg

(r)**Indonesian cucumber salad** *(Atjar ketimun)*

Hot pepper paste *(Sambal ulek)*

Fried bananas with coconut or vanilla ice cream

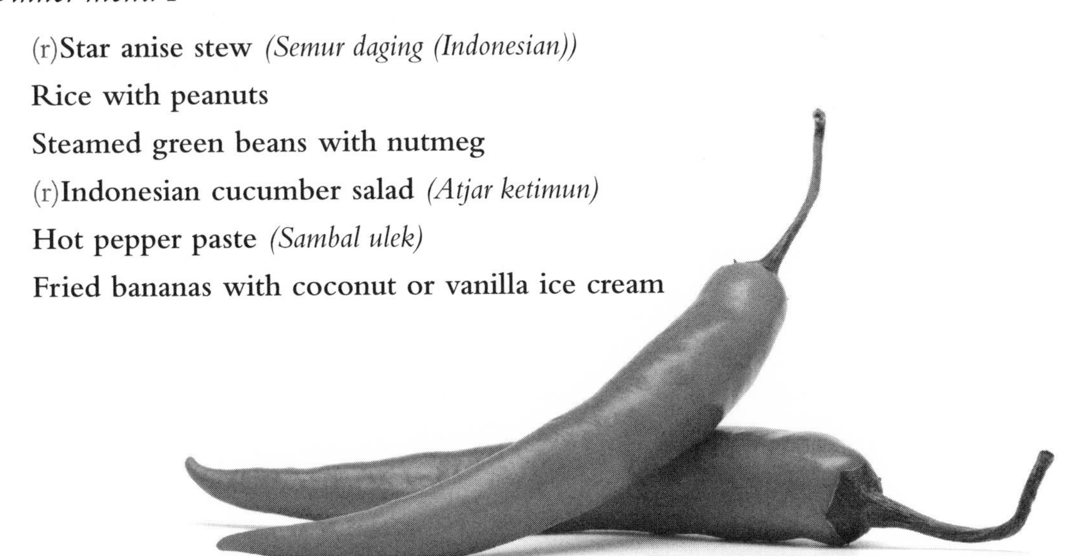

Star anise stew (SEMUR DAGING (INDONESIAN))

Note: Indonesian sweet soy sauce can be found in Asian or Dutch specialty stores. If not available, whisk together ½ cup regular soy sauce and ½ cup molasses as a substitute.

2 tablespoons oil
1 medium yellow onion, chopped
3 cloves garlic, minced
8 whole cloves
1 teaspoon dried ginger
4 star anise
1 teaspoon granulated sugar
1½ teaspoons finely textured salt
Freshly ground black pepper
2 pounds stew beef
5 tablespoons Indonesian sweet soy sauce *(ketjap manis)*
8 tablespoons water

Heat the oil in a large saucepan over medium heat and sauté onion and garlic until light brown. Stir in cloves, ginger, star anise, sugar, salt, and pepper. Add beef, and note, no browning is necessary. Pour *ketjap manis* and water over everything. cover the pan tightly, and simmer gently for about 1 hour, making sure the mixture does not cook dry. The beef should be very tender, if necessary cook a little longer. Yield: 6 servings.

Indonesian cucumber salad (ATJAR KETIMUN)

2 cucumbers, peeled, seeded, cut lengthwise in half, then into chunks
½ cup white distilled vinegar
8 whole peppercorns
1 teaspoon dried hot red pepper flakes
1 bay leaf
1 tablespoon packed dark brown sugar

Place cucumber chunks in a bowl. In a saucepan over medium heat, boil vinegar and remaining ingredients for 3 minutes. Pour sauce over cucumber, and cool. Cover and refrigerate. Serve cold. Make on the day of your dinner. Yield: 6 servings.

Dinner menu II

The first course of this menu holds a sweet surprise—the mushrooms and eggs are flavored with fresh orange juice. Most people who have eaten this dish are astonished how well these flavors combine! The recipe comes from Dutch-American Anne (Stevenson) van Cortlandt (1774-1821), and it originally called for claret, but I prefer to use sherry. The dessert is a delicious coconut cake with apricots.

(r)**Mushroom fricassee with orange**

(r)**Cod with mustard sauce** *(Kabeljauw met mosterdsaus)*

Broccoli and cauliflower and/or carrots

Potatoes, mashed or boiled

(r)**Apricot-coconut squares** *(Abrikozentaart met kokos)*

Mushroom fricassee with orange

1½ pounds mushrooms, cleaned and sliced

2 tablespoons salted butter

1 medium yellow onion, finely chopped

¾ teaspoon minced fresh (or scant ¼ teaspoon dried) marjoram

¾ teaspoon minced fresh (or scant ¼ teaspoon dried) thyme, leaves only

Salt and freshly ground black pepper

4 eggs

3 tablespoons good red wine or dry sherry

1 orange, juiced

¼ teaspoon freshly grated nutmeg

2 or 3 tablespoons beef or lamb roast juice, if available

In a large frying pan over low heat, warm mushrooms until they give off all their juices. Drain, and discard liquid. Wash and dry pan, and over medium heat, add butter and let it color lightly. Stir in mushrooms, onion, marjoram, and thyme. Season with salt and pepper and sauté for a few minutes until onions become translucent. In a small bowl, beat together eggs, wine or sherry, orange juice, nutmeg, and meat juice, if available. Reduce heat to low, and pour egg mixture over mushrooms and wait until eggs set somewhat before stirring. The mixture will thicken and look more or less like scrambled eggs. The original recipe suggests serving this recipe in a dish rubbed with shallots with a garnish of lemon or orange wedges. I serve this with some greens lightly dressed with vinaigrette, perhaps a crusty roll, and a small glass of the same wine or sherry used in the dish. Yield: 6 small servings.

Cod with mustard sauce (KABELJAUW MET MOSTERDSAUS)

The main course is another typically Dutch dish. Thick, white fish, no matter what kind, is often served like this.

6 fresh cod fillets, or thawed if frozen

Water

Finely textured salt, optional to taste

2 teaspoons Old Bay seasoning, optional

4 tablespoons salted butter

¼ cup all-purpose flour

2 tablespoons whole-grain mustard

Place fillets in a shallow pan big enough to hold the fish in one layer. Add enough water to come up halfway to the top of the fish. Sprinkle with salt and Old Bay, if desired. Cover the pan and poach gently over medium heat until done, when fish can be flaked. Remove the fish to a heated platter and keep warm. To make the sauce, measure 2 cups of the poaching liquid, adding warm water if necessary. In a saucepan, melt butter, stirring flour in vigorously all at once. Slowly add poaching liquid. Continue stirring until sauce becomes smooth. Finally add mustard, taste, and adjust seasonings if necessary. Spoon some of the mustard sauce over the fish, and serve the rest in a dish on the side. Yield: 6 servings.

Apricot-coconut squares (ABRIKOZENTAART MET KOKOS)

1 package (7-ounce) sweetened coconut, divided

½ pound (2 sticks) unsalted butter

½ teaspoon finely textured salt

1 cup granulated sugar

5 eggs

Scant ½ cup whole milk

2 cups self-rising flour

20 apricot halves or more, drained if using canned

Reserve ½ cup coconut from the package and set aside. Preheat oven to 350°F. In an electric mixer, beat butter, salt, and sugar on high for about 3 minutes, or until light and fluffy. Add eggs one at a time and incorporate before adding next egg. Stir in milk, and use a spatula in an under-over motion to gently combine remaining coconut and flour a little at a time. Spoon batter into a buttered 9x13-inch baking dish, and tap with the back of a wooden spoon. Layer apricots cut side down in four even rows and sprinkle with reserved coconut. Bake for about 45 to 50 minutes, or until golden brown and when a toothpick inserted comes out clean. Cool on a rack, and cut into squares. Serve as is, or with a dollop of whipped cream or vanilla ice cream. Yield: 20 squares.

Dinner menu III

In this little menu, start the meal with three hors d'oeuvres chosen from the recipes in chapter 9. For example, make a plate for each guest and include shrimp salad in a plum tomato, a deviled egg, and a toast triangle with mackerel paté. If you wish, add mixed greens with vinaigrette dressing and place on the table before seating guests. Serve the main course family-style. Many supermarkets sell bags of ready-to-eat chestnuts, which can simply be mixed with cooked and seasoned brussels sprouts, and heated through. If none are available, use canned whole chestnuts.

Little hors d'oeuvres plate from chapter 9 (see above)

(r)**Orange-hazelnut crusted chicken breasts** *(Kippeborst met hazelnootkorst)*

Brussels sprouts with chestnuts

Homemade applesauce

Potatoes

(r)**Mother's pudding**

Orange/hazelnut crusted chicken breasts

(KIPPEBORST MET HAZELNOOTKORST)

This recipe is my adaptation of one in the 1683 edition of *De Verstandige Kok (The Sensible Cook)*. It has been adapted in various ways by many authors and cooks, including the chef of the wonderful restaurant De Kas in Amsterdam. In the original recipe, the chicken is stewed whole with orange peels and sugar, and dusted with cinnamon before serving.

1 orange, zested

½ cup finely chopped hazelnuts

½ cup Panko or plain bread crumbs

2 pounds boneless, skinless chicken breasts

Finely textured salt and freshly ground black pepper

1 egg, beaten lightly with a fork

Oil, for frying

1 orange, juiced

White wine, preferably Riesling or Sauvignon Blanc, if needed

Ground cinnamon, for dusting

In a shallow bowl, combine zest, hazelnuts, and bread crumbs. Set aside. Cut chicken breasts in half horizontally. Cover them with plastic wrap, and using gentle taps with the flat side of a mallet, flatten them to about ¼-inch thickness. Season with salt and pepper, and brush each chicken piece with beaten egg, then coat with the zest-hazelnut mixture.

In a large frying pan over medium heat fry chicken pieces in 2 tablespoons of oil for 2 to 3 minutes, flip over and fry the other side, covered for 1 to 2 minutes. If necessary fry chicken in batches, adding more oil as needed. When done, return chicken to pan and add orange juice. If the liquid does not cover the bottom of the pan, add a little wine. Cover the pan, and cook chicken on medium to low heat for 5 minutes or until an internal temperature of 165°F is reached using an instant-read thermometer. Remove to a heated platter and dust each chicken piece lightly with cinnamon. Yield: 6 servings.

Mother's pudding

My mother served some sort of cornstarch or "*maizena*" pudding with fruit compote and cream every Sunday. Sometimes she added sliced cake and sprinkled it with a little liqueur—a handy way to use up stale cake. Lots of sweetened whipped cream is essential to the success of the dish, which of course is delicious! Also keep in mind the colors of the fruit you choose—for example, a mixed red berry compote looks very nice with the yellow pudding and the white cream. The pudding can be made a day ahead.

FOR THE PUDDING:

4 cups (1 quart) whole milk, divided

1 vanilla bean, seeds scraped

⅓ cup plus 2 tablespoons granulated sugar

½ cup plus 3 level tablespoons cornstarch

2 eggs, beaten lightly with a fork

FOR THE FRUIT COMPOTE:

10 ounces mixed red berries or any kind of fresh, frozen, canned, or dried fruit

1-2 tablespoons granulated sugar

FOR FINAL ASSEMBLY:

Plain cake, such as pound cake, sliced

3 or 4 tablespoons fruit liqueur

½-1 pint heavy cream, whipped with 3 teaspoons granulated sugar

MAKE THE PUDDING: Rinse a medium saucepan with water. Set aside ½ cup milk for diluting cornstarch. In the saucepan over low heat, combine milk, vanilla bean pod, and seeds. Bring milk to a boil slowly in order to give the vanilla bean time to release its flavor about 7 to 8 minutes or until boiling. In a small bowl, combine cornstarch and sugar, and whisk in eggs and milk until a smooth sauce forms. After milk boils, take pan off the burner, add a little hot milk to sauce, and stir to combine. Return the pan to the burner, reduce the heat, and pour sauce into hot milk. Stir constantly until it thickens. Cook 3 more minutes, stirring to remove starchy flavor. Remove vanilla bean pod. Rinse a bowl with cold water and pour pudding in, cover with plastic wrap to prevent a skin from forming. Cool, then refrigerate.

MAKE THE FRUIT COMPOTE: In a large saucepan over medium heat, cook fruit with sugar for 2-3 minutes for frozen or canned fruits; dried fruits need to be cooked until softened, about 10-12 minutes.

TO ASSEMBLE: In a pretty glass bowl, spoon a layer of pudding then sliced plain cake. Drizzle cake with some appropriate liqueur—Chambord, a raspberry liqueur, goes well with berries—if desired. Top with most of the fruit, then half the cream and another pudding layer. Finish with the remaining cream and spoon on the last of the fruit. Yield: 6 to 8 servings

Festive tree-lighting dinner

I grew up with a tree with candles at Christmastime, and my husband, Don, and I have continued that tradition. Trees with candles, rather than electric lights, are not so common anymore in the United States or the Netherlands, but once you see one, you love the romance of it. "Isn't it dangerous?" is the first question people ask. The answer is, "No, not if you're careful." Let's face it, accidents happen to trees with electric lights as well. The candles are affixed to the tree branches in metal candleholders with clips, and Don does make sure a fire extinguisher is handy. Someone is always in the room while the tree is lit. In the 45 years we have done this, we never have had any problems.

Usually we decorate the tree in the second weekend of December, and invite some friends for dinner the following week to see it lit for the first time. There is something magical about a tree lit this way, and friends happily join us to see it. Sometimes we burn the candles only half way, and re-light on a subsequent occasion, but other times we go to the very end. Myth has it that if you watch the last candle burn out and make a wish, the wish comes true.

You don't have to have candles in the tree to have a tree-lighting party. Electric lights are beautiful too, and the first time a tree is lit is always an occasion for oohs and aahs. The main course recipe of the menu for a tree-lighting evening comes from a hand-written cookbook of the Philips family, dated 1847. Anton Philips was the founder of the world-famous Philips (Norelco) factories of Eindhoven in the latter half of the nineteenth century. This dish was a favorite for Sunday dinner, hence the name Sunday cabbage. It takes about 25 minutes to prepare, and needs 2 hours to cook. Plenty of time for you to do other things.You'll see it is well worth the trouble, and a perfect dish for a dinner party, since it can easily wait until you're ready to serve. Use savoy cabbage for ease in preparation.

Menu for a tree-lighting dinner

Green salad with blue cheese, and hazelnuts with vinaigrette dressing (use your favorite)

(r)**Sunday cabbage** *(Zondagse kool)*

Carrots and parsnips

Small boiled potatoes with chopped parsley and melted butter

Apple custard (chapter 5, see page 45)

Sunday cabbage (ZONDAGSE KOOL)

1 (2-pound) head savoy or green cabbage, thoroughly washed, leaf by leaf

2 pounds ground beef or veal

3 thick slices bread, crust removed,

½ cup whole milk or water

2 eggs

1 medium yellow onion, minced

2 teaspoons finely textured salt

¼ teaspoon freshly ground black pepper

¼ teaspoon freshly grated nutmeg

Bring a large pot of water to a boil over medium heat and drop in separated cabbage leaves to wilt them, about 3 to 5 minutes. Remove them from the water with tongs and cool. Save the water in the pot. Bring water back to a boil. In a bowl, soak bread slices in milk, then squeeze fairly dry. In a large bowl, combine ground beef with bread, eggs, onion, and seasonings. Knead with your hands until mixture is well-combined. Rinse a clean tea towel or napkin to remove soapy residue and wring dry. Place towel in a bowl, then place the outside cabbage leaves in it. Cover with a thin layer of meat mixture, add cabbage leaves, then meat, and repeat until all ingredients have been used up, ending with a layer of cabbage. Tie the cloth together with kitchen twine to form a ball. Carefully slide this bundle into the boiling water, and tie it to the handle of the pot. Do not let any part of the cloth hang over the side of the pan. Gently cook cabbage for 2 hours. Remove it slowly and place it in a colander set in a large bowl. Allow cabbage to drain for 5 minutes. Open the cloth and carefully remove what will look like a whole steamed cabbage. Place in a serving bowl or on a rimmed platter. To serve: cut into wedges at the table. Yield: 6 to 8 servings.

Festive December buffet

In setting up a buffet, I like to use the dessert as centerpiece. Presented on a footed serving piece, it adds drama to the table and people will know what is coming for what is still for most the favorite course. Set up your buffet table in the middle of the room, so guests can walk around it. Take a moment and walk yourself through the order in which the food will be presented so that your table is arranged in a logical fashion.

After many years of party planning, I have learned that you will need three times more ice and twice as many paper napkins and mixers than you think you need. Choose recycled paper napkins, so you will not feel so bad using so many. Keep ice to be used in drinks separate from ice used for chilling. Ice that comes into contact with bottles or cans might not be clean. Buy flavored seltzers for mixers by the case, since it is more economical and you surely can use leftovers at a later date in the holiday season. Some quick rules of thumb: A fifth of liquor will give you 17 (1½-ounce) drinks; a liter, which is about 34 ounces, will make 22. A standard wine bottle is 750 milliliters, which yields 4 (6-ounce) glasses. White and pink wines are served chilled; so are dry and medium sherries and light red wines such as Beaujolais; red wines are served at room temperature, preferably between 65°F and 68°F.

A very important side note when having guests over: Whatever bathrooms will mostly be used, make sure they are spotless. Remove all personal articles, set out clean towels, a box of tissues, and have plenty of toilet paper on hand. Think ahead where the coats will go—if they go in your bedroom, make the bed.

Menu for a festive December buffet

(r)**Mustard soup** (*Mosterdsoep*)

Smoked salmon with capers and diced red onion

Sliced turkey

Sliced ham

Poached cored pear halves, hollows filled with cranberry compote

Mixed green salad with your favorite dressing

(r)**Coleslaw with hot butter dressing** *(Koolsla)*

Christmas bread (from chapter 5)

Assorted breads or rolls

Butter, herb butter (from chapter 9) **mayonnaise, and mustard**

(r)**Rice pudding with white wine and currants (***Rijstebrij met krenten)*

Clementines

Cookies (from chapter 6)

Store-bought or homemade chocolates (from recipes in chapter 5)

Mustard soup (MOSTERDSOEP)

This soup is very popular in the Netherlands. Restaurants use the mustards of their town or region to vary the flavors. If no Dutch mustards are available, use a whole-grain variety. Mustard gets its name from the fact that it originally was made from must (freshly pressed grape juice not yet fermented into wine) and mustard seeds, either *Brassica juncea* (brown/black), or *Brassica hirta* (white/blond) and sometimes from a combination of both.

3 tablespoons salted butter

1 large shallot, finely chopped

3 tablespoons flour

4 cups chicken broth

3 tablespoons Dutch or Dijon grainy mustard

1 cup whole milk

1 cup half-and-half

¼-½ teaspoon finely textured salt, as needed

¼ teaspoon freshly ground black pepper

¼-½ teaspoon turmeric, optional for color

In a large saucepan with a heavy bottom, melt butter over medium heat, add shallot and sprinkle in flour. Cook, stirring constantly, until lightly browned. Whisk in chicken stock and mustard and simmer for 30 minutes. Add milk and half-and-half and simmer for a few more minutes. Taste and adjust seasonings with more mustard, salt and freshly ground pepper. Stir in turmeric to improve the color, if desired. Yield: 6 servings.

Coleslaw with hot butter dressing (KOOLSLA)

This recipe cannot be repeated enough. It is the way the early Dutch settlers of New Netherland—now the states of New York, New Jersey, Delaware, and parts of Pennsylvania and Connecticut—served their coleslaw, and I must say still my favorite way.

2 cups julienned green cabbage

2 cups julienned red cabbage

⅓ cup white wine vinegar

¼ cup melted salted butter

Salt and freshly ground black pepper

Combine all ingredients well ahead of dinnertime so that the flavors can marry, but do not refrigerate or butter will congeal.

Rice pudding with wine and currants (RIJSTEBRIJ MET KRENTEN)

1⅓ cups short-grain rice

2 Granny Smith apples (about 1 pound), peeled, cored and diced

¾ cup currants (see note, page 46)

2 cups fruity white wine

4 tablespoons salted butter

⅓ cup granulated sugar

1 teaspoon ground cinnamon

Half-and-half or heavy cream

Combine rice, apples, currants, and wine in a large saucepan and bring to a boil. Reduce heat to low, cover the pan and gently simmer until the rice is done, about 45 minutes. Check occasionally to see it did not cook dry, if so add more wine. When the rice is done, take off the heat stir in the butter, sugar, cinnamon, and as much half-and-half or cream to make a consistency you like. Yield: 10 to 12 servings.

Festive December Dutch breakfast

Every American friend who has been to the Netherlands always tells me "I love those big Dutch breakfasts!" They are indeed a hearty start to the day, and here is a menu. Instead of the Dutch version of French toast and the omelet, you could just serve boiled eggs plus the other items. However, since both are easy to make, I think you'll enjoy adding them, particularly the toast, which is baked in the oven. For those who don't know, a Holland rusk is a round, dry biscuit, or twice-baked bread, similar to the *zweiback,* which is a form of rusk eaten in Germany, but not as hard.

(r)**French toast, the Dutch way (***Wentelteefjes)*

Homemade applesauce

(r)**Farmer's omelet** *(Boerenomelet)*

Cheese

Cold-cut platter

Jam and or hazelnut spread (I use Nutella brand)

Salted butter

Whole-grain bread

Holland rusks, if available

Raisin bread (or the Christmas bread from chapter 5, see page 50)

French toast, the Dutch way (WENTELTEEFJES)

The beauty of this French toast is that it can be made in the oven, and frees up your stovetop when you're busy making the omelet and other things. This recipe can easily be doubled.

1 tablespoon melted salted butter

4 eggs and 1 egg white

¼ teaspoon ground cinnamon

4 slices good country bread

Good quality syrup, optional

Preheat oven to 450°F. Brush a baking sheet with melted butter. In a flat dish, whisk eggs, egg white, and cinnamon. Soak bread slices for 1 minute on each side, and place on buttered baking sheet. Bake for 5 to 7 minutes, until light brown. Turn them over and bake for another 3 to 4 minutes. Remove and serve with or without syrup, or if you prefer with some fruit on top. Yield: 4 servings.

Farmer's omelet (BOERENOMELET)

The following omelet would frequently be our Saturday evening meal when I was young. I don't know why really, but I must say I loved it. Of course, it works well for a big American breakfast.

4 small cooked potatoes (fingerlings are very good for this), sliced

3 scallions with their greens, finely chopped

1 tablespoon salted butter

Farmer's omelet

1 tablespoon vegetable oil

2 to 3 tablespoons parsley and chives, chopped

3 thick slices bacon, cooked in the microwave until crispy, crumbled

3 slices sandwich ham, cut into small pieces

2 ounces (about 4 tablespoons) young or medium aged Gouda cheese, cubed

6 eggs, beaten with a whisk

Finely textured salt and freshly ground black pepper, to taste

In a 9-inch omelet pan over medium heat, fry potatoes and scallions in butter and oil until light brown. Stir in parsley, chives if used, crumbled bacon, ham, and cheese cubes. Pour in whisked eggs, and season with salt and pepper. Reduce heat to low, and cook omelet on one side only, until the top is solidified and cooked. If you can, slide the omelet onto a platter. If that's too difficult, cut it into wedges and transfer to the platter. Yield: 6 servings.

Festive Christmas tea

For the last 35 years or so, I have given a Christmas tea on the first Monday in December. I invite 10 of my best friends and make it as festive an occasion as I can manage. One year, I gave everyone a hat and gloves that I had found in various thrift and antique shops. Last year, I found 10 different decanters and filled them with homemade Hippocras. This year, everyone will get a candy dish with homemade chocolates. I look forward to the day all year, and so do my friends, they tell me. This day is really about friendships and good memories.

Here is my menu. I vary it from year to year, but keep the same three sandwich fillings every year.

(r)**Chicken and almond sandwiches** *(Kip met amandeln sandwiches)*

(r)**Kippered herring sandwiches** *(Gerookte haring sandwiches)*

(r)**Chip's cucumber sandwiches** *(Chip's komkommer sandwiches)*

3 or 4 different cookies (from chapters 5 and 6)

1 or 2 chocolates (from homemade chocolates in chapter 5)

Marzipan figures (from chapter 4)

Quince squares (from chapter 5)

Pear tart (from chapter 5)

Served with black and herbal teas

Hippocras (chapter 10, see page 113) is served at the end of the party as a toast to the beginning of the holiday season or the beginning of Delicious December!

Chicken and almond sandwiches

(KIP MET AMANDEL SANDWICHES)

2 cups cooked chicken, finely diced

2 tablespoons celery, finely chopped

2 tablespoons scallions, finely chopped

3-4 tablespoons slivered almonds

4 tablespoons good-quality mayonnaise

1 lemon, juiced

Finely textured salt and freshly ground black pepper, to taste

8-10 slices buttered thinly sliced white sandwich bread

In a bowl, combine chicken, celery, scallions, and almonds with mayonnaise. Taste and add as much lemon juice, salt, and pepper as necessary. Liberally fill sandwiches, remove crusts and cut into squares or diamonds. Yield: 4 to 5 sandwiches, or 16 to 20 squares.

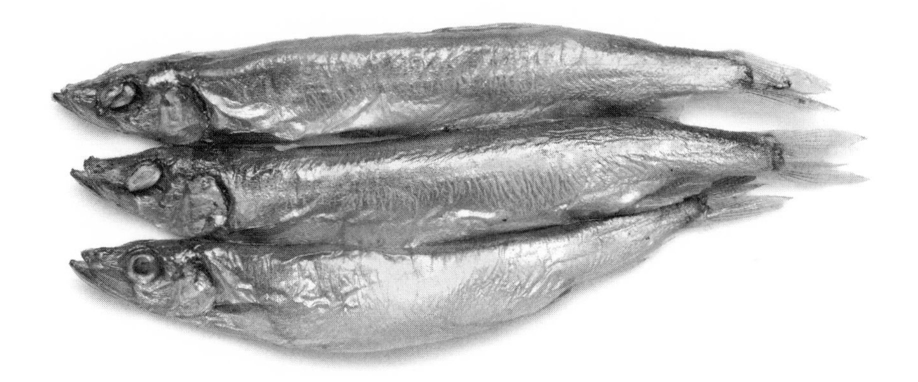

Kippered herring sandwiches (GEROOKTE HARING SANDWICHES)

1 (3.25-ounce) can kippered or smoked herring

1 hard-boiled egg

1 tablespoon minced scallion

2-3 tablespoons good-quality mayonnaise

6-8 slices buttered thinly sliced whole wheat sandwich bread

In a small bowl, mash herring and any liquid from the can with egg and scallion. Add enough mayonnaise to make a spreadable consistency. Liberally fill sandwiches, remove crusts, and cut into squares or diamonds. Yield: 3 to 4 sandwiches, or 12 to 16 squares.

Chip's cucumber sandwiches (KOMKOMMER SANDWICHES)

My friend Mary Beth (Chip) Kass usually makes these sandwiches for my tea. She always comes early that day to help me finish any last-minute details.

Finely textured salt

1 long European cucumber, peeled and thinly sliced

8-10 slices buttered thinly sliced white sandwich bread

Salt cucumber slices and let stand at least 1 hour. Carefully drain and pat dry with paper towels. Place cucumber on buttered bread slices. Top with another slice, remove crusts. Yield: 4 to 5 sandwiches, or 16 to 20 pieces.

Children's tea party

I had a tea party with two little girls recently, and concluded it would be a very nice event to have in the days between Christmas and New Year's when all the excitement has died down and life seems dull suddenly. Don't be mistaken, little boys like tea parties too! What follows is the menu I made for them. Since it was at lunchtime, the rule was they had to eat one sandwich, so four pieces, and then they could "attack" the sweets. It worked well, though they did not like the cucumber sandwiches, so I have suggested thinly sliced apple drizzled with a bit of honey as an alternative. The cheese sandwiches can be cut into all sorts of animal shapes, and they were a big hit. The others I simply cut into squares or triangles.

Menu for children's tea party

Use spreadable cheese (such as Laughing Cow) for the sandwiches and cut them into animal shapes with cookie cutters.

Cheese sandwiches

Turkey sandwiches

Cucumber or sliced apple and honey sandwiches

3 different small cookies (from chapter 6)

Small candies, Hershey's chocolate kisses, M&Ms, or similar

Weak tea or ginger ale, served from a child's tea set

Happy Holidays to all, and enjoy a Delicious December!

Websites and Mail-Order Sources

Before I give you my favorite websites and mail-order sources, here is a USDA website for sterilizing jars: nchfp.uga.edu/publications/publications_usda.html

If you google "Dutch mail order stores," you will get a strange assortment of offerings, ranging from brides, pharmaceutical products (including marijuana), fireworks, yachting, and boating accessories, along with a few Dutch food stores. The easiest way to find the latest sources (plus a lot more interesting current information about the Dutch) is to go to the online newsletter www.dutchinamerica.com.

• Vander Veen's The Dutch Store, 2755 28th Street SW, Wyoming, MI, 49519. They have many products and their prices are very reasonable, including the shipping cost. www.vanderveensdutchstore.com

• Kaas & Company – A Taste of Holland, 83 Washington Street, Norwalk, CT, 06854 www.kaasnco.com

• Kingma's Market, 2225 Painfield Ave., Grand Rapids, MI, 49505; (616) 363-7575; www.kingma'smarket.com. I order by telephone 7-pound tubs of almond paste.

• Jaarsma Bakery, 727 Franklin St., Pella, IA, 50219; (641) 628-2940; www.jaarsmabakery.com. This bakery with a long history makes Dutch letters and assorted Dutch pastries.

• Don't miss the Dutch website www.knutselidee.nl. It is the very best site for finding ideas for ingeniously packaged presents. Even if you do not read Dutch, the pictures will help you. Click on every item on the homepage for lots of inventive concepts.

• If you want to buy a Moravian star, go to www.hernhuttersterren.nl.

• Go to my website www.peterrose.com and click on Peter's Picks for Hudson Valley products.

• For books go to www.GoDutch.com.

• For information on the Dutch experience in early America, go to www.nnp.org, a site created by the New Netherland Institute in Albany, NY.

• For a visual depiction of the early period, go to www.lftantillo.com. Len Tantillo is a well-known Hudson Valley painter, known for his paintings of early Dutch settlements, the Half Moon (Henry Hudson's ship), and Fort Orange.

I hope this information will help you to get started!

Credits

xiv Replica of seventeenth-century cake board with image of Saint Nicholas

2 Nineteenth-century icon of Saint Nicholas, surrounded by twelve pictures of his life and miracles (Courtesy W.J. van Vloten)

4–5 *The Charity of Saint Nicholas*, Cornelis de Vos (1584 – 1651). (Courtesy Museum Ons Lieve Heer op Solder, Amsterdam, the Netherlands)

8 *The Feast of Saint Nicholas*, Jan Steen (1626 – 1679). (Courtesy Rijksmuseum, Amsterdam, the Netherlands)

10 *The Saint Nicholas Celebration*, Cornelis Dusart (1660 – 1704). (Courtesy Atlas van Stolk, Rotterdam, the Netherlands)

13 Maria van Rensselaer's account with Wouter Albertsz. Van den Uythoff, de backer [the baker], 1676. (Courtesy New York State Library, Manuscripts and Special Collections, Albany, New York)

16 Saint Nicholas arrives in Rotterdam by boat. (Courtesy photographer Bas Czerwinski)

Index of Recipes

About the Author

PETER G. ROSE has published numerous articles and books on Dutch, Dutch American, and Hudson Valley cuisine, including *Summer Pleasures, Winter Pleasures: A Hudson Valley Cookbook*, also published by SUNY Press; *Food, Drink and Celebrations of the Hudson Valley Dutch*; *The Sensible Cook: Dutch Foodways in the Old and the New World*; and *Foods of the Hudson: A Seasonal Sampling of the Region's Bounty*. She is the coauthor (with Donna R. Barnes) of both *Matters of Taste: Food and Drink in Seventeenth-Century Dutch Art and Life* and *Childhood Pleasures: Dutch Children in the Seventeenth Century*. In 2002 she was the recipient of the Alice P. Kenney Award for research and writing on the food customs and diet of the Dutch settlers in New Netherland. She lives in South Salem, New York.

For more information about the author, please visit www.peterrose.com.